75
Ensemble
Warm-Ups

75 Ensemble Warm-Ups

Activities for Bands, Choirs, and Orchestras

Phyllis S. Weikart

Beverly Boardman

Elisabeth Bryant

Published by

HIGH/SCOPE® PRESS
A division of the High/Scope Educational Research Foundation
600 North River Street
Ypsilanti, Michigan 48198-2898
(734)485-2000, FAX (734)485-0704
Web site: *www.highscope.org*   E-mail: *press@highscope.org*

Editor: Linda Koopmann
Cover design, text design: Judy Seling of Seling Design

Library of Congress Cataloging-in-Publication Data

Weikart, Phyllis S., 1931-
    75 ensemble warm-ups : learning on the move : grades 6 [to] 12 /
Phyllis S. Weikart, Beverly Boardman, Elisabeth Bryant ; with forewords
by Malcolm Rowell, Jr. and Elizabeth Power.
        p. cm.
Glossary: p.
Includes bibliographical references (p.   ) and index.
    ISBN 1-57379-144-X (soft cover : alk. paper)
    1. Ensemble playing--Instruction and study. 2. School
music--Instruction and study. 3. Music rehearsals. I. Title: Seventy
five ensemble warm-ups. II. Boardman, Beverly. III. Bryant, Elisabeth.
IV. Title.
    MT810.W352 2003
    781.4'38'071--dc22
                                    2003021695

Printed in the United States of America

10 9 8 7 6 5 4 3 2 1

Catalog number M1024

Contents

4 Pitch and Melody   79

8 Expressive Qualities 147

Foreword

It is with great pleasure that I endorse *75 Ensemble Warm-Ups,* a book that will enhance teaching effectiveness and student learning. Through greater depth of musical understanding, the ensemble experience will offer both the teacher and the student greater rewards.

75 Ensemble Warm-Ups is a proactive program of learning that allows the student to engage in the creative aspects of music-making in addition to the sequential development and refinement of executive skills. The concepts addressed in this method creatively engage students in the learning process as they experience steady beat, tone quality, phrase, listening, form, dynamics, meter, style, and texture. Students are motivated when they achieve musical results. The authors of this book offer a series of curricular exercises to be used as "warm-ups" to develop musicianship and musical independence, while embracing important musical values.

This important method book is thoughtfully written by three exceptional musicians and movement educators who approach the teaching of musicianship through movement-based active learning. Their concepts will improve teaching, facilitate musical understanding, open minds and ears, encourage ownership, and result in performances of greater depth of musical understanding. I look forward to using it with my ensembles!

Malcolm W. Rowell, Jr.
Professor of Music
Director of Bands
University of Massachusetts–Amherst

I consider it a great privilege to have seen firsthand the power of the teaching principles of movement and music. The Florida West Coast Symphony Youth Orchestra and *Summer at the Symphony* participants have been experiencing this movement-based active learning approach to music for nearly a decade, and it is evident.

Students have exhibited accelerated development in musicianship skills that not only have enriched their ability to play their instruments but also, and perhaps more importantly, have enabled them to understand the aesthetic values of music.

The ideas presented in this book will encourage other young musicians to feel the joy and excitement in learning that comes when music concepts are brought to life. Though outcomes are an essential reason to employ specific practices, it is also important to remember the spirit in which these practices are used. Our students are not only learning. They like the approach because it is fun!

Elizabeth Power, Education Director
Florida West Coast Symphony

Acknowledgments

We have looked forward to writing this book for many years, and we thank the High/Scope Foundation for making it possible. As a trio of authors, we have enjoyed working together on this book and are excited about the possibilities it presents to music educators. We would like to acknowledge the following people who have helped with this endeavor, all of whom are dedicated professionals in the field of education: Jessica Wilke and Kathleen Kane for providing ideas for the warm-ups and valuable assistance; Jay Hunsberger and Malcolm Rowell for their motivating and supportive responses and for providing the ultimate model in conducting; and our friends and colleagues in the *Education Through Movement* network for listening to our ideas and providing feedback.

We want to extend our appreciation to Linda Koopmann, our editor, for her ability to organize our thoughts throughout the book; to Pattie McDonald, our editorial assistant, for her meticulous entry of revisions; to Judy Seling of Seling Design for her eye-catching cover and interior design; to Lynn Taylor for her careful layout of the book; and to Malcolm Rowell and Elizabeth Power for their extremely supportive forewords to the book. Many thanks also go to Karen Sawyers, Assistant Director of High/Scope's Movement and Music Division, for her insight and caring, and for keeping us on task. Without her help, this book might never have been published.

Two of us would like to acknowledge co-author Phyllis Weikart, Director of the Movement and Music Division at High/Scope. She is a good friend, mentor, and colleague, and we are grateful for her outstanding example of master teaching and her constant dedication to the field of movement and music. *Education through Movement* is special to all of us and invaluable to learners around the world.

75
Ensemble
Warm-Ups

Introduction

This idea book is a resource of short, movement-based rehearsal warm-ups for conductors and directors of a variety of vocal and instrumental ensembles—from upper elementary choirs, Orff ensembles, and beginning bands to middle school and high school choirs, orchestras, and bands. Because of their focus on basic music concepts, these lesson plans also can be used with church ensembles and in private studios for voice, piano, and other instruments.

Active start-ups to ensemble rehearsals lead to more productive sessions. Imagine a rehearsal where student musicians are engaged, motivated, empowered, and excited about performing; where they are able to respond immediately to every gesture of the conductor or director; where they have such a complete understanding of musical concepts that they can successfully interpret repertoire without continual reinforcement. The warm-ups in this book will help youth ensemble conductors and directors create the kind of learning environment in which these experiences are possible.

Guiding Principles for Planning Successful Ensemble Experiences

Many ensemble students—whether beginners or more experienced—have difficulty remembering dynamics, for example, or performing a phrase more musically, because they have not experienced and understood abstract musical concepts in their simplest form. The warm-ups in this book are designed to make these abstract concepts more concrete. Warm-ups are grouped by chapter based on the following broad concepts:

- *Steady beat*—The success of any ensemble depends upon each individual's ability to maintain steady beat independently. The internalized feel of steady beat provides the foundation for all musical experiences.

- **Rhythm**—Steady beat is essential for rhythmic precision. This precision requires "feel" on the part of the performer. If a performer is able to use a single neutral syllable such as *bah* or *bom* to speak the rhythm (instead of using numbers or words that have meaning), while also keeping steady beat with body movements, the performer has achieved the first step to rhythmic precision. (Neutral syllables such as *bah* and *bom* have no meaning. They are used by Dr. Edwin Gordon, noted music learning theorist, to allow students to focus on feeling the rhythm rather than looking for the right word to label it.)

- **Pitch and melody**—The accurate performance of melody depends upon hearing and identifying pitches. Using movement to represent pitch direction makes the abstract concept of melody concrete. In addition to the movement, both instrumentalists and vocalists need to use a single neutral syllable (*bah* or *bom*) to sing their parts. This allows them to focus on the melody rather than on the words or note names.

- **Harmony**—Hearing and understanding chord progressions and hearing one's own part within the overall harmonic structure of the music are integral skills in building a quality ensemble. Experiencing parts and chord progressions through movement helps build the student's understanding and awareness of concepts
  necessary to develop these skills.

- **Phrase**—Phrase is the combination of beat, rhythm, and melody in a horizontal line. In order to perform musically, the ensemble needs to feel the duration of a phrase and be able to communicate this through performance. Since phrase involves space and time, movement is essential for concrete understanding.

- **Form**—Understanding the framework of a musical selection is essential to its performance. When performers can analyze the structure of a piece of music, they begin to recognize repeated sections, and this saves rehearsal time. Musicians can gain an understanding of form by the use of movement to illustrate phrases or sections that are the same or different.

- **Expressive qualities**—The qualities of dynamics, tempo, articulation, rubato, and balance are important but abstract concepts. They help bring the music to life and are important to the final performance. Experiencing a rubato section through movement, for example, results in a much more complete rendering of the music.

Introduction to the Warm-Ups

Chapter one of this book outlines High/Scope's *Movement-Based Active Learning Process*. An understanding of this process is integral to the successful implementation of all the experiences described in later chapters. Through the *Movement-Based Active Learning Process* students are instantly engaged in action, thought, and language. They are encouraged to share ideas and discuss them. Although this may take more time initially, the payoff comes when students gain ownership of concepts that they can transfer to the rehearsal and performance of all repertoire.

Chapters two through eight present ensemble warm-ups that illustrate seven musical concepts. Each warm-up uses the *Movement-Based Active Learning Process* described in chapter one as the foundation for success.

How warm-ups are organized

Within each chapter, warm-ups appear in order of difficulty, from easiest to more difficult. All warm-ups can be simplified or extended to meet the needs of both experienced and inexperienced groups. To achieve success in implementing the warm-up ideas, follow the tips listed below and use the warm-ups in many varied ways.

Ten Tips for Conductors

1) *Start where your learners are,* not where you want them to be.
2) *Use any combination of small groups* or partners where appropriate.
3) *Adapt a particular lesson* for your available space as needed.
4) *Engage all musicians,* even when rehearsing only one section of the ensemble.
5) Note that *explore* is the first step in most lesson plans.
6) Have instrumentalists *sing parts* before playing.
7) Use *neutral syllables (bah, bom)* to sing or speak parts before using numbers, solfeggio, or words.
8) *Use neutral syllables to speak rhythms* while keeping steady beat on the body for rhythmic precision.
9) *Reinforce ideas* through folk dance.
10) *Simplify or extend ideas* to meet the needs of your ensembles.

To use an idea only once and expect musicians to understand and own the concept is unrealistic.

Although adult leaders of bands and choirs are usually referred to as directors rather than conductors, for consistency and clarity we have referred to all adult ensemble leaders throughout the warm-ups as conductors.

Warm-up components include:

- **Possible key experiences:** The High/Scope movement and music key experiences that relate to individual warm-ups are listed at the top of the first page of each warm-up.

- **Materials:** Materials to use in each activity are listed next, including appropriate selections from High/Scope's *Rhythmically Moving 1–9* (RM; Weikart, 2003a) or *Changing Directions 1–6* (CD; Weikart, 1990) series of musical recordings. Many of these selections are included in the compact disk provided with this book.

- **Check for understanding:** This warm-up component begins with two preparatory actions conductors should take before explaining a warm-up— *ask about students' understanding of the concept* and *assess students' ability.* The knowledge gained from these two actions allows you to start the warm-ups where your students are in their understanding of the musical concept.

- **Experience the concept:** Suggested steps to follow in presenting the warm-up activity are described in this component. You may wish to omit some steps or include others not listed, depending on the environment and ability levels of your students. We urge you to include the exploration phase of the activity when suggested.

- **Facilitate and reflect:** This warm-up component contains sample questions you may pose to your students. They are included because it is our philosophy that thought and language must be added to action to help students reach true ownership of movement, music, and curriculum concepts. The specific questions you use, of course, will depend on the experience of your students. You do not need to ask all of them.

- **Apply to ensemble/repertoire:** This component provides the transition between experiencing music concepts and applying those concepts directly to the current repertoire of the ensemble. A couple of examples of direct application are provided with the intent that the conductor will then develop his/her own examples specific to particular pieces of music.

- **Extend the experience:** Extensions are suggested ways to expand, modify, or simplify the warm-up activity to make it more meaningful for your particular ensemble.

- **Related warm-ups:** This warm-up component directs you to specific preceding warm-ups that ensembles should master before attempting another particular warm-up. Related warm-ups that follow later in a chapter or in following chapters are also listed.

* * *

Using movement-based active learning for your rehearsals will open doors you never thought existed and provide experiences you never thought possible. The ideas presented in this book are only the beginning of new and exciting opportunities as you and your ensembles discover and create different experiences that fit your own needs. Good luck and have fun!

A Movement-Based Active Learning Process

Education Through Movement: Building the Foundation, a program of High/Scope's Movement and Music Education Division, consists of the following four components:

- Key experiences in movement and music
- Movement core
- Teaching model
- Active learning support strategies

This is the delivery system—the "how to"—that teachers and conductors who are trained in High/Scope's *Movement-Based Active Learning Process* keep in mind as they facilitate their ensembles' learning and performance. **The process considers ensemble members and conductors to be partners,** mutual initiators and supporters of learning. This idea of shared control of practice sessions will be explained in more detail as each of the four components of movement-based active learning are discussed.

High/Scope's Key Experiences in Movement and Music

High/Scope's key experiences in movement and music, one component of the *Movement-Based Active Learning Process,* are activities that High/Scope has identified as being most beneficial to a young person's development in the areas of movement and music. We have not listed all of the *music key experiences* in this book, but we have included those that supply important connections for specific ensemble warm-ups. A complete list and detailed discussion of the key experi-

Key Experiences in Movement

Key Experience	Concept
Acting upon movement directions	Seeing and perceiving; hearing and comprehending; feeling and identifying
Describing movement	Thinking ability and language use (moving and describing; planning; recalling; linking movement with a word—SAY & DO Process)
Moving in nonlocomotor ways	Achieving comfort and awareness of anchored movement in personal space
Moving in locomotor ways	Achieving comfort and awareness of non-anchored movement in personal and general space
Moving in integrated ways	Achieving comfort with and awareness of non-locomotor and locomotor movement purposefully combined
Moving with objects (instrument)	Achieving comfort with and awareness of non-locomotor, locomotor, and integrated movement when using an object
Expressing creativity in movement	Extending movement by using one's own ideas
Feeling and expressing steady beat	Ability to independently express and maintain steady beat
Moving in sequences to a common beat	Ability to sequence movement

ences in music are found in *Foundations in Elementary Education: Music* (Carlton & Weikart, 1994). Since the movement key experiences are the base for all other activities in the process, however, we briefly define them below.

In the movement key experiences, movement is purposeful. Intent is expressed through decision making, planning, imitating, doing, and recalling. We use these key experiences to recognize, support, and extend each student's fundamental abilities in order to achieve success and understanding focused on enhancing the ensemble's performance.

Keeping these nine movement key experiences in mind helps conductors to concentrate on working with and improving the final performance. Are student performers attending to what is said? Do they comprehend what is heard or seen? What about creativity and problem solving? Are they competent with steady beat and with sequences of movement in steady beat? Through the use of the

Movement-Based Active Learning Process, ensemble members can be encouraged to lead, to share their ideas, and to follow another member's suggestions.

The Movement Core

The movement core illustrated in the diagrams below is the motor-development base for purposeful movement for people of all ages in the *Education Through Movement* program. Note that one of the diagrams is labeled *nonlocomotor,* and the other is labeled *locomotor.* Nonlocomotor movement is movement performed in place without shifting weight from the supporting foot, for example, patting, swinging, and twisting movements. Locomotor movement is movement performed while shifting weight from foot to foot, for example, marching.

During nonlocomotor (no weight shifting) movement at any age, moving both sides of the body symmetrically (for example, moving both arms in the same direction) at the same time is easiest. In contrast, during locomotor (weight shifting) movement, alternating movement from side to side is easiest (for example, stepping in place or walking about the space).

Movement complexity is illustrated in the center circle of these diagrams from top to bottom, with the easiest organization of the body at the top and the most complex organization of the body at the bottom. *One side...other side* refers to movement in repetition on one side of the body and then on the other side. This type of movement allows development to occur on each side of the body. Very

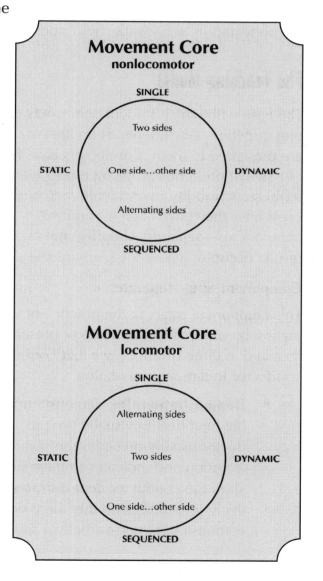

often, an individual's non-preferred side of the body is weaker than the preferred side, or lacks the same degree of coordination possessed by the more preferred side. Conductors introducing movement to a population of any age should keep in mind this simple-to-complex way of moving.

The words placed around the circle of each movement core diagram refer to the ways in which the body executes purposeful movement. *Single movements* are those that have one action performed over and over. *Sequenced movements* are those that have two or more actions sequenced, for example, the act of fingering an instrument. *Static movements* are those that pause in the desired location, and *dynamic movements* are those that keep going. Remembering this organization of the body and its actions can help students experience success.

The Teaching Model

The ease with which student performers grasp movement demonstration or interpret directions often depends on the way in which the directions or demonstrations are presented to them. Conductors have found that the *Education Through Movement* program's teaching model leads to increased success, a sense of personal responsibility in ensemble members, and a decreased need to re-teach concepts after they have been introduced. A close look at each of the model's three components—**separate, simplify, and facilitate**—will explain why such favorable results occur.

Component one—separate

This component refers to the practice of initiating experiences or presenting information by using only one mode of presentation at a time. Sensory information is received in three distinct ways that correspond to the following three modes of conductor initiation/presentation:

- **Demonstration.** The demonstration mode of presentation requires ensemble members to visually process information in order to respond. The conductor usually precedes the demonstration with a statement that gains their attention and indicates to them that the conductor is going to demonstrate. Then the conductor ***demonstrates without speaking.*** Many tasks are effectively presented with this silent demonstration method (for example, demonstrating non-verbally a specific fingering or a specific action used while conducting). When a specific way of doing a movement is desired, it helps to demonstrate it rather than to use verbal directions.

- **Verbal (spoken or sung) directions.** Verbal directions require students to process auditory rather than visual information in order to respond. Conductors usually precede the verbal presentation with a statement such as, "Please listen and follow these directions." The statement lets an individual know that directions are going to follow. Then the conductor *tells* ensemble members what is needed or what to do *without demonstrating.*

- **Hands-on guidance.** The conductor uses hands-on guidance to silently assist an individual. Hands-on guidance and verbal directions do not occur at the same time.

By choosing to *separate* one of these three modes of presentation and use it alone at any given time, the conductor enables student performers to focus on a single message and process information more quickly and more accurately. Combining one or more modes of presentation (for example, expecting ensemble members to watch you conduct and listen to what you say at the same time) usually gives students too much sensory input. Instead of integrating the input from different senses, some will naturally use their strongest learning modality and block out information from the other senses, or worse yet, miss the information entirely because of the confusion caused by using two senses at once.

Component two—simplify

The conductor using this component begins with what is easy or manageable to process, so that all ensemble members can become immediately engaged and experience success. To use this component, the conductor must first consider each student's present capabilities, based on the conductor's knowledge of prerequisite skills, and then determine the sub-tasks that make up the task at hand. Taking these things into account allows the conductor to begin where the ensemble is able to function.

Observing student performers when they are with a partner or in a small group can help you select and promote active learning experiences. Occasionally, conductors express concern that using the *simplify* strategy slows them down, but using this component is well worth a few extra minutes if it results in the ensemble attaining quality of performance.

Component three—facilitate

The first two components of the teaching model, *separate* and *simplify,* are strategies that conductors use in presenting concepts and in planning and initiating activities. The third and last component of the teaching model, the *facilitate* strategy, concerns the ways in which conductors engage students through thought and language, thus supporting and furthering their ability.

Conductors facilitate when they encourage ensemble members to initiate their own ideas and experiences. They facilitate when they give them time to explore concepts on their own, with partners, or in small groups, planning and making choices about how they will solve problems and applying existing knowledge to a task.

Conductors also facilitate when they supply language and when they listen and respond to language that students use among themselves. Asking them to talk about what they are planning to do, to describe what they are doing, and to recall and reflect on what they did are other ways to facilitate. Finally, providing a safe, interactive environment where conductors and ensemble members work as partners and support one another is the most important way for conductors to further their ensemble's learning.

Active Learning Support Strategies

Dictionary definitions of the word *teach* often include phrases such as "to impart knowledge or skills," or to "show or help to learn." Of these phrases, the most significant to us is "help to learn." These words suggest the **conductor's facilitative role** and the **conductor/learner partnership** that is central to the success of the ensemble. We believe the conductor's role is not to direct activities and dispense information alone, but to encourage an **active learning approach** that engages student performers in their own search for understanding. Individuals who are absorbed in a learning task usually display an energy and zeal that is often lacking in conductor-directed situations. We are looking to change ensemble members from passive receivers of information to active constructors of their own knowledge and ability. "Teaching does not imply learning" (Weikart, 2003b).

The conductor both introduces ideas and recognizes opportunities to support and extend ideas initiated by students. Because *to do* is *to understand,* this initiation of ideas by both conductor and ensemble member is supported across the band, orchestra, or choir. Ensemble members make choices, share ideas, and talk about their experiences to promote greater awareness of concepts. The following are basic strategies of the actual learning approach as developed in the *Education Through Movement* program:

- **Initiation by teacher and students** is critical to successful learning. When student initiation is incorporated, teachers find that students generally maintain high interest.

- **Exploration of purposeful movement** leads to true understanding and the ability to apply concepts. Purposeful movement is used for exploration because there is thought and intention used.

- **Choices and planning by students** enable them to be actively involved in the process. Students take on ownership of the task and its solutions.

- **Language listened to and supplied** implies much verbal interaction as ensemble members supply language and listen to others. Conversations occur among students and between the conductor and students.

- **Facilitation and reflection** encourage band, orchestra, and choir members to reflect on their experiences, to draw conclusions, to think about other ways they might have proceeded, and to think of what made the experience hard or difficult. This facilitation and reflection helps conductors determine if further experiences are necessary to achieve success.

- **Support from conductors and peers** implies creating a supportive environment so members feel they have a say in their own learning. Providing a positive, supportive rehearsal atmosphere means realizing that conductors and students are on the educational journey together; each person brings something valid. No one who tries is ever completely wrong.

Summary

Four very important aspects of the ensemble environment have been described in this chapter. **The key experiences in movement and music, movement core, teaching model,** and **active learning support strategies** taken together might be said to constitute a way that a conductor can inspire or *lead from behind*. The signs of this kind of leadership are obvious. Conductors inspire ensemble members when they encourage them to:

- **Explore ideas** rather than passively accept what the conductor dictates.

- **Lead and make choices** instead of always following the conductor's lead and choices.
- **Feel free to express ideas** instead of thinking that they can only speak when asked a question by the conductor.
- **Initiate experiences** instead of always following along with conductor-directed experiences.
- **Feel safe in trying and making mistakes** instead of always needing to have everything "right."
- **Respond to positive, descriptive statements from the conductor** instead of individual, judgmental praise.
- **Respond to a conductor's comforting voice quality** instead of responding only when they hear forceful, threatening language.

We believe that any teaching/learning situation functions best when learners feel that they are given responsibility for learning, when they are respected and acknowledged for their contributions, and when learners do not feel threatened or frightened. Frightened or punished learners do not learn! Keep in mind that "teaching does not imply learning," and the lack of a partnership in learning diminishes the end result (Weikart, 2003b).

Steady Beat

Mastering the warm-ups in this chapter will allow each member of the ensemble to become competent in *basic timing*. Competence in basic timing is the ability to independently feel and keep the underlying steady beat of a rhyme, song, or a recorded or live musical selection and express it with nonlocomotor and locomotor movement.

This independence of beat will allow the musician to be successful in synchronizing beat with the ensemble, understanding and working with meter, performing accurate rhythms, and understanding and following conducting patterns.

Warm-Ups 1–16

1. Starting and stopping together
2. Developing steady beat independence
3. Synchronizing ensemble beat
4. Understanding *macrobeat* and *microbeat**
5. Applying macrobeat and microbeat knowledge
6. Working with macrobeat and microbeat through *chair dancing***
7. Using the macrobeat to prevent rushing
8. Feeling accented offbeats
9. Performing entrances in time
10. Understanding the organization of duple (2 or 4) meter
11. Understanding the organization of triple (3) meter
12. Feeling and identifying duple meter versus triple meter

Macrobeat and *microbeat* are terms used by music learning theorist Dr. Edwin Gordon. See Glossary for definitions.

**Chair dancing* is a concept developed by Phyllis Weikart. In a chair dance, participants remain seated and move their feet as if they were standing up and dancing. The seated position gives students the opportunity to work out the pattern more easily.

13. Beginning uncommon meter
14. Understanding simple meter versus compound meter
15. Exploring conducting movements
16. Working with conducting patterns

Warm-Up Tips

- All warm-ups can be simplified or extended to meet the needs of your ensembles.
- Keeping silent beat without copying another person is the ultimate goal in keeping a beat. Only then is steady beat truly independent.
- This process provides "real-time" assessment (active, nonwritten assessment).
- Start where your learners are, not where you want them to be.
- When working with steady beat, use instrumental recordings so attention can be focused on the beat and not on lyrics.

Possible Key Experiences
Moving in nonlocomotor ways
Moving in locomotor ways
Acting upon movement directions

1 Starting and stopping together

Materials

None

Check for understanding

Ask pertinent questions: Ask students to describe what a conductor shows a group through his or her movements, expressions, and comments.

Assess ability: Ask the ensemble to start and stop a given pitch by following your visual cues.

Experience the concept

Each student explores ways to start and stop while using nonlocomotor and loco-motor movements. They each share one idea with another student who copies the idea and describes the movement he or she makes.

In groups of two, students explore ways to give visual and verbal cues to start and stop the movements.

In small groups, each student gives a visual or verbal cue to the group to start or stop a movement or a sound.

Facilitate and reflect

What challenges did you face when you led a group? What challenges did you face when you tried to follow the leaders?

What are the advantages of visual cueing? What are the advantages of verbal cueing?

Apply to ensemble/repertoire

A number of student conductors start and stop the entire ensemble as it performs scales or warm-ups.

The conductor starts and stops the entire ensemble as it performs a portion of current repertoire.

Extend the experience

The ensemble performs a selection from current repertoire that contains frequent transitions. Students respond to various conductors.

The ensemble starts and stops without a conductor.

Related warm-ups

Following this warm-up:

- Performing entrances in time (warm-up 9)

- Exploring conducting movements (warm-up 15)

Possible Key Experiences
Feeling and expresssing steady beat
Acting upon movement directions

2 Developing steady beat independence

Materials

"Jessie Polka" (RM 8)

Other musical recordings that show a strong steady beat, such as "Mechol Hagat" (RM 4) and "La Bastringue" (CD 2)

Check for understanding

Ask pertinent questions: Ask students to define the term *steady beat.*

Assess ability: Ask students to find and keep individual steady beat by stepping in place to two musical recordings that have different metronome markings.

Experience the concept

Each student explores ways to keep a steady beat by using an upper body movement such as knee-patting. Students share with the whole group the movements they used, and each person copies different ideas in his or her own timing.

Students do the same as above, but make sure that the beat is *silent* (make beat movements in the air without touching anything).

Students explore ways to keep individual steady beat while standing and alternating their feet, as in marching. They share ideas, copy them in their own timing, and describe them first verbally and then by keeping the beat silent (using silent movements).

Facilitate and reflect

What are some characteristics of steady beat?

What are some of the strategies you used to match someone else's beat?

Why is individual internal steady beat important to the performance of music?

Apply to ensemble/repertoire

Students listen to a variety of musical recordings. They find and keep a silent steady beat.

Half of the ensemble plays a selection from current repertoire, and the other half keeps a silent steady beat while using either nonlocomotor (anchored) or locomotor (nonanchored) movements.

Extend the experience

Students form groups of two. Partners in each group copy each other's steady-beat movements, first with sound and then silently.

In groups of four, students each find a silent steady beat by using either the upper body or a stepping movement. Each person in the group copies how each of the other group members keeps steady beat. Groups put beat movements together with a musical selection.

Related warm-ups

Following this warm-up:

- Synchronizing ensemble beat (warm-up 3)
- Understanding macrobeat and microbeat (warm-up 4)

3 Synchronizing ensemble beat

Materials

None

Check for understanding

Ask pertinent questions: Ask students to tell what they know about ensemble timing.

Assess ability: Ask each student to keep an independent silent steady beat movement. Each student then synchronizes beat with the rest of the ensemble until the ensemble is on one common beat.

Experience the concept

With a partner, students explore ways to synchronize steady beat. They share ideas and try out different strategies with the whole ensemble.

Students explore ways to synchronize a silent steady beat with a partner. They share, describe, and try different strategies with the group.

One student begins a silent steady beat movement, and the rest of the ensemble joins in with the same timing and movement.

Facilitate and reflect

What were the differences between keeping steady beat with sound versus with silence?

What kind of beat do you keep while playing instruments or singing?

What did you do to find the ensemble beat/timing?

How does finding an ensemble beat apply to the performance of a musical selection?

Apply to ensemble/repertoire

Different students use a steady beat movement to lead the ensemble. The ensemble moves to the given steady beat and then applies that beat to scales or other warm-ups.

Different students lead the group in performing various selections from the ensemble's current repertoire. The focus is on whether the group follows the conductor's timing.

Extend the experience

The conductor, or student conductor, starts a selection from the ensemble's current repertoire at a given tempo, then drops out while the ensemble continues performing. This can be done to different tempi.

Various sections of the ensemble perform a portion of the current repertoire without a conductor, and the rest of the group assesses the accuracy of the timing (beat).

Related warm-ups

Preceding the warm-up:

- Developing steady beat independence (warm-up 2)

Following the warm-up:

- Exploring conducting movements (warm-up 15)

Possible Key Experiences
Moving in nonlocomotor ways
Moving in locomotor ways
Feeling and expressing steady beat

4 Understanding macrobeat and microbeat

Materials

"Alley Cat" (RM 3)

Other musical recordings that illustrate steady beat, such as "Cherkessiya" (RM 2) and "Al Gemali" (CD 4)

Check for understanding

Ask pertinent questions: Ask students to tell what they know about macrobeat and microbeat.

Assess ability: Ask students to try to feel the macrobeat and microbeat in a musical recording.

Experience the concept

Students listen to a musical recording or sing a familiar song. Students explore different steady-beat movements and share and copy ideas.

Students and the conductor define and discuss macrobeat and microbeat relationships. One student demonstrates an approximate *macrobeat* tempo, and another student demonstrates an appropriate *microbeat* tempo simultaneously, using movement. The ensemble copies, and students describe the relationship.

Students form groups of two. The first partner in a group initiates either macrobeat or microbeat to a song or a musical recording. The second partner copies and identifies macrobeat or microbeat. Partners switch roles and repeat the above two steps, using the beat not used the first time around.

Facilitate and reflect

What is the relationship of macrobeat to microbeat?

How do macrobeat and microbeat apply to the ensemble performance?

Apply to ensemble/repertoire

A student begins a conducting pattern, and the ensemble performs a given warm-up using that beat. The ensemble identifies whether it is macrobeat or microbeat.

Different students conduct a selection from the ensemble's current repertoire, using macrobeat and microbeat movements.

Extend the experience

The ensemble finds macrobeat or microbeat movements while using different meters.

Half of the ensemble performs a current selection while the other half keeps macrobeat or microbeat.

Related warm-ups

Preceding this warm-up:

- Developing steady beat independence (warm-up 2)
- Synchronizing ensemble beat (warm-up 3)

Following this warm-up:

- Applying macrobeat and microbeat knowledge (warm-up 5)

5 Applying macrobeat and microbeat knowledge

Materials

"Jessie Polka" (RM 8)

Other musical recordings, such as "Sicilian Tarantella" (RM 6) and "Alley Cat" (RM 3)

Check for understanding

Ask pertinent questions: Ask students to tell what they know about performing macrobeat and microbeat.

Assess ability: Ask students to keep microbeat, then macrobeat, to a musical recording.

Experience the concept

Students break up into small groups, explore movements, and create imaginary "machines" that have moving parts in a relationship of macrobeat tempo to microbeat tempo. For example, one person in a group swings his or her arms to an approximate *macrobeat* tempo. A second person makes a physical connection to the first person (by holding hands or linking arms, and so on) and steps an approximate *microbeat* tempo. A third person connects to the "machine" and bends his or her knees in an approximate *macrobeat* tempo, and so on. Students then add vocal sounds to each movement.

Students share their machines with the whole group.

Facilitate and reflect

What part of this machine shows macrobeat? What part shows microbeat?

Why is it important to be able to keep macrobeat while others are keeping microbeat?

Apply to ensemble/repertoire

Students identify areas in current repertoire where one ensemble section performs microbeat while another performs macrobeat.

Students perform warm-ups in which part of the group is using macrobeat and the other part of the group is using microbeat.

Extend the experience

Students create machines that show the duration of particular note values in a given meter.

Students create machines in different meters.

Related warm-ups

Preceding this warm-up:

- Developing steady beat independence (warm-up 2)
- Understanding macrobeat and microbeat (warm-up 4)

Following this warm-up:

- Working with macrobeat and microbeat through chair dancing (warm-up 6)
- Using the macrobeat to prevent rushing (warm-up 7)

6 Working with macrobeat and microbeat through chair dancing

Materials

"Tipsy" (RM 6) and "Good Old Days" (RM 6)

Other musical recordings, such as "Popcorn" (RM 7)

Check for understanding

Ask pertinent questions: Ask students to tell what they know (or remember) about macrobeat and microbeat.

Assess ability: Ask the ensemble to feel and maintain the macrobeat and microbeat in the musical recording "Tipsy" (RM 6). Watch for accuracy.

Experience the concept

Students explore ways to move their feet first in microbeat tempo and then in macrobeat tempo while they are seated. Partners copy and describe the movements.

The conductor teaches the chair dance to the tune of "Good Old Days" (RM 6).

Facilitate and reflect

In the dance "Good Old Days," where and how were microbeats and macrobeats used?

What is the relationship of microbeat to macrobeat?

Apply to ensemble/repertoire

Using a selection from current repertoire, half the group performs, while the other half creates foot movements to macrobeat or microbeat while remaining seated.

Students look at a section from current repertoire and mark the macrobeats in microbeats on their individual parts with pencil.

Extend the experience

The ensemble uses other examples of microbeat and macrobeat chair dancing movements that are found in *Teaching Movement and Dance,* fifth edition (Weikart, 2003b).

Students choreograph a chair dance by using macrobeat and microbeat movements.

Related warm-ups

Preceding this warm-up:

- Developing steady beat independence (warm-up 2)
- Understanding macrobeat and microbeat (warm-up 4)
- Applying macrobeat and microbeat knowledge (warm-up 5)

Following this warm-up:

- Using the macrobeat to prevent rushing (warm-up 7)

Possible Key Experiences
Moving in nonlocomotor ways
Feeling and expressing steady beat

7 Using the macrobeat to prevent rushing

Materials

None

Check for understanding

Ask pertinent questions: Ask students to define the term *macrobeat* and explain what is meant by the phrase *rushing the beat.*

Assess ability: N/A

Experience the concept

Students divide into small groups and explore using their hands to keep an approximate macrobeat tempo.

Each small group uses a neutral syllable (*bah* or *bom*) to speak a steady macrobeat tempo and performs the rhythm from a chosen piece of ensemble repertoire.

Facilitate and reflect

What strategies did you use to set and keep the macrobeat tempo while speaking rhythm patterns?

How did keeping the macrobeat help you stay in tempo?

Apply to ensemble/repertoire

Someone in the ensemble sets a macrobeat, and the rest of the ensemble performs a selection from current repertoire and follows that beat and tempo.

Half of the ensemble students keep a macrobeat with their hands, while the other half copies the macrobeat movement and performs a selection from current repertoire that uses that beat. The two groups then switch roles.

Extend the experience

Students pat an approximate microbeat tempo, alternating their hands. They add a variety of spoken rhymes. While patting, they add foot movements in the same tempo and continue to speak the rhythm patterns.

Students repeat the above extension, patting and stepping macrobeat.

Related warm-ups

Preceding this warm-up:

- Developing steady beat independence (warm-up 2)

- Understanding macrobeat and microbeat (warm-up 4)

Following this warm-up:

- Strategies for increasing tempo (warm-up 64)

8 Feeling accented offbeats

Materials

"Tipsy" (RM 6)

Other musical recordings that illustrate accented offbeats, such as "Dirlada" (RM 5) and "Bossa Nova" (RM 7)

Check for understanding

Ask pertinent questions: Ask students to tell what they know about offbeats and accents.

Assess ability: Play a musical recording and ask students to pat the beat that they feel is stressed.

Experience the concept

Students step microbeat to a musical recording (for example, "Tipsy," RM 6), adding pats on the macrobeat simultaneously. While their feet remain in the microbeat, students change the pat to pat-clap-pat-clap. (At this point, both feet and upper body are on microbeat.) Students keep their feet stepping in microbeat, but remove the pat in the upper body, leaving only the claps on the offbeats.

The patterns shown in the beat boxes on the next page illustrate microbeat, macrobeat, and accented offbeat. The ensemble compares the boxes with offbeat accents to those with accents on the beat and discusses differences.

Students create different rhythm patterns to layer on over accented offbeats.

Facilitate and reflect

How does the accented offbeat feel different from other beat organizations?

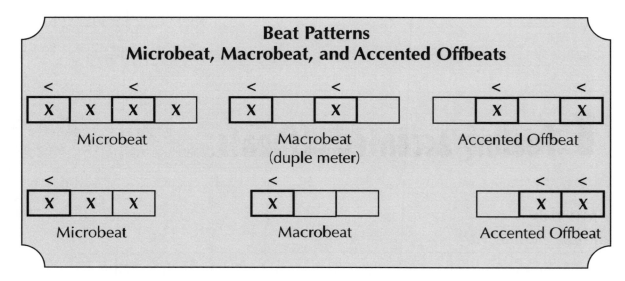

Beat Patterns
Microbeat, Macrobeat, and Accented Offbeats

What types of music use accented offbeats?

Apply to ensemble/repertoire

Students identify sections of current repertoire that use accented offbeats.

Half of the ensemble performs sections from current repertoire, and the other half steps with the accented offbeats.

Extend the experience

The conductor asks the percussion section to keep every microbeat, while the ensemble steps with accented offbeats.

The ensemble plays musical recordings, some that use offbeat (jazz, rock, and so on) and some that use regular accents. Students identify which selections use accented offbeats and discuss what the offbeats do to the music.

Related warm-ups

Preceding this warm-up:

- Developing steady beat independence (warm-up 2)
- Synchronizing ensemble beat (warm-up 3)

Following this warm-up:

- Understanding the organization of duple meter (warm-up 10)

9 Performing entrances in time

Materials

None

Check for understanding

Ask pertinent questions: Ask students to explain how to perform entrances on time.

Assess ability: Start and stop the ensemble several times and check for accuracy.

Experience the concept

Small groups of students create four-beat nonlocomotor movement sequences, labeling them with language (the *SAY & DO Process* described in the Glossary). Students choose one of the four-beat movement sequences and practice it in group time.

Two of the small groups join together and decide on the number of times that each group will perform its four-beat sequence. The first group performs its sequence while the second group keeps a macrobeat. The second group performs its sequence while the first group keeps a macrobeat, entering as soon as the first group finishes.

Facilitate and reflect

What strategies do you use to make an entrance on time?

Is it harder to make vocal or instrumental entrances on time? Why?

Apply to ensemble/repertoire

The conductor divides a scale into two groups of four notes. The ensemble forms two groups, with each group performing one group of four notes. Groups alternate playing their group of notes.

The two groups perform the same activity, but each group plays every two notes this time and then alternates on every note.

In a selection from current repertoire, students find a section that has many entrances. They play or sing that section and perform entrances accurately.

Extend the experience

Students listen to recordings of instrumental and choral music (from the ensemble's collection) and determine whether the entrances are made accurately.

Students sing a round or canon and focus on accurate entrances.

Related warm-ups

Preceding this warm-up:

- Starting and stopping together (warm-up 1)

- Developing steady beat independence (warm-up 2)

- Synchronizing ensemble beat (warm-up 3)

Following this warm-up:

- Working with conducting patterns (warm-up 16)

10 Understanding the organization of duple (2 or 4) meter

Materials

Musical recordings such as "Hora Nirkoda" (CD 1), "Irish Washerwoman" (RM 3), and "D'Hammerschmiedsg'sell'n" (RM 7)

Check for understanding

Ask pertinent questions: Ask students to tell what they know about duple meter.

Assess ability: Ask students to demonstrate macrobeat and microbeat to recorded music in duple meter.

Experience the concept

With a partner (or in small groups), students explore macrobeat and microbeat movements to a recorded musical selection. They share ideas, copy each other's movements, describe the movements, and identify whether they are macrobeat or microbeat.

The first student in a group demonstrates an approximate walking microbeat tempo. The second student in the group layers on a macrobeat hand movement (one macrobeat for every two microbeats).

Each student performs microbeat foot movements and macrobeat hand movements simultaneously.

Facilitate and reflect

What can you say about the organization of microbeats and macrobeats in duple meter?

What are some time signatures in duple meter?

How can you tell whether the music is in duple or triple meter?

Apply to ensemble/repertoire

Students identify current repertoire in duple meter.

A student conductor leads the ensemble in warm-ups in duple meter. The same student conductor leads in the microbeat, and the ensemble performs in the macrobeat.

Extend the experience

Students listen to musical selections in various styles and meters and identify those that are in duple meter.

The conductor leads the ensemble in a simple song, such as "Mary Had a Little Lamb," in duple and then triple meter. The ensemble discusses the difference in feel and manner of performing.

Related warm-ups

Preceding this warm-up:

- Understanding macrobeat and microbeat (warm-up 4)

Following this warm-up:

- Understanding the organization of triple meter (warm-up 11)
- Working with conducting patterns (warm-up 16)

11 Understanding the organization of triple (3) meter

Materials

"Mechol Hagat" (RM 4) and "D'Hammerschmiedsg'sell'n" (RM 7)

Other musical recordings in duple and triple (or other) meter, such as "Hora de la Rişipiţi" (CD 5) and "Gaelic Waltz" (RM 1)

Check for understanding

Ask pertinent questions: Ask students to tell what they know about triple meter.

Assess ability: Ask students to demonstrate microbeat and macrobeat to recorded music in triple meter.

Experience the concept

Students explore walking approximate microbeats and patting macrobeats; they put microbeats into groups of three.

Students form groups of two. The first partner in a group sets an approximate microbeat walking tempo. The second partner pats one macrobeat for every three walking microbeats. Partners switch roles.

Facilitate and reflect

Is it easier to show microbeat or macrobeat?

How does triple meter feel different from duple meter?

Can you think of any familiar songs in triple meter?

Apply to ensemble/repertoire

Students perform scales in durations/patterns that reflect triple meter.

Students perform current repertoire in triple meter while keeping macrobeat with their feet.

Extend the experience

Students create more challenging microbeat movement sequences in triple meter (for example, knees, head, head).

Related warm-ups

Preceding this warm-up:

- Understanding macrobeat and microbeat (warm-up 4)

- Understanding the organization of duple meter (warm-up 10)

Following this warm-up:

- Feeling and identifying duple meter versus triple meter (warm-up 12)

- Beginning uncommon meter (warm-up 13)

- Working with conducting patterns (warm-up 16)

12 Feeling and identifying duple meter versus triple meter

Materials

Pencils

Any kind of drum

"Sulam Ya'akov" (CD 2) and "Danish Masquerade" (CD 4)

Other musical recordings, such as "Popcorn" (RM 7)

Check for understanding

Ask pertinent questions: Ask students to define the term *meter.*

Assess ability: Ask students to listen to two different musical recordings and identify whether the music is in duple or triple meter.

Experience the concept

Students walk to the beat of a drum and explore ways to react to random accents through movement (for example, by jumping on the accents).

Students walk to the beat of a drum, react to accents organized into two, three, or four beats in a group, and name the meter.

Students create movements to "Danish Masquerade" (3 sections in duple, triple, duple) as they decide whether sections are in duple or triple meter. Movements should demonstrate the meter.

Facilitate and reflect

How can you tell the difference between duple and triple meter?

How does knowing the meter help with ensemble performance?

Apply to ensemble/repertoire

Students choose sections from current repertoire and determine the meter. They perform the sections, exaggerating the accents at the beginning of each measure.

Half of the ensemble performs a section from current repertoire, while the other half listens and determines the meter.

Extend the experience

Students explore and create their own conducting patterns to show duple and triple meters. Various students volunteer to conduct the ensemble, using their own ideas.

The ensemble identifies the meter.

Students listen to a pre-selected musical recording, determine the meter, and create hand-movement patterns to go with each.

Related warm-ups

Preceding this warm-up:

- Developing steady beat independence (warm-up 2)
- Understanding the organization of duple meter (warm-up 10)
- Understanding the organization of triple meter (warm-up 11)

Following this warm-up:

- Beginning uncommon meter (warm-up 13)

13 Beginning uncommon meter

Materials

"Ivanica" (CD 3)

Other musical recordings in uncommon meter, such as "Lemonaki" (CD 3) and "Tsakonikos" (RM 9)

Check for understanding

Ask pertinent questions: Ask students to define the term *uncommon meter.*

Assess ability. N/A

Experience the concept

Students explore ways to move in steady beat, creating beat groupings through the use of accents.

Students step to the steady beat performed on a drum by a student leader.

The student leader adds accents to create duple meter. Students decide how notes are grouped and add movement to the accented beat. They repeat the process in triple meter.

Alone or in twos, students explore ways to combine duple and triple groupings to create uncommon meter. Students share their beat grouping combinations, copy each other's patterns, and describe their movements.

Facilitate and reflect

How is uncommon meter created?

What is the difference in feel between common meter and uncommon meter?

Apply to ensemble/repertoire

Students find examples of uncommon meter in selections from current repertoire. They discover how notes are grouped and play the piece with groupings in mind.

Students listen to an example of uncommon meter and create movement to the macrobeats.

Extend the experience

Students pat accents to 5/8 meter on their laps by using beat groupings of 2 + 3 or 3 + 2. Students then layer on the rhythm used in one phrase from current repertoire, by speaking the rhythm in neutral syllables (*bah, bom*) over the accents.

Students take a well-known easy melody or song in a common meter and change it into an uncommon meter. They sing or play in the common meter, then the uncommon meter.

Related warm-ups

Preceding this warm-up:

- Developing steady beat independence (warm-up 2)
- Understanding the organization of duple meter (warm-up 10)
- Understanding the organization of triple meter (warm-up 11)

Following this warm-up:

- Working with conducting patterns (warm-up 16)
- Working with uncommon meters through subdivision (warm-up 27)

Possible Key Experiences

Moving in nonlocomotor ways
Moving in locomotor ways
Feeling and expressing steady beat
Feeling and identifying meter

14 Understanding simple meter versus compound meter

Materials

"Mechol Hagat" (RM 4) and "Irish Washerwoman" (RM 3)

Other musical recordings that illustrate simple and compound meters, such as "Bat Arad" (CD 1) and "Rustemul" (CD 5)

Check for understanding

Ask pertinent questions: Ask students to tell what they know about simple or compound meters.

Assess ability: N/A

Experience the concept

Students explore approximate microbeat walking tempo with feet or hands and by speaking a duple, then a triple, subdivision.

Students form groups of two. The first partner in a pair conducts a two-, three-, or four-beat pattern. The second partner copies and layers on a subdivision with mouth sounds. Partners discuss and label the sounds, then switch roles.

The first partner in a group initiates a subdivision with mouth sounds. The second partner conducts and organizes it into a simple or compound meter. Partners discuss and label, then switch roles, using the meter not used the first time around.

Facilitate and reflect

Which meter signatures or rhythm values are simple? Which ones are compound?

How do simple meters feel to you? How do compound meters feel to you?

Compare and contrast 2/4, 6/8 (3/4, 9/8...)

Apply to ensemble/repertoire

The ensemble performs a subdivision. A student conducts, organizing the beat into simple or compound meter. The group labels the beat with some body-part movement or action or with sound.

Students label selections from current repertoire as simple or compound meter.

Extend the experience

The conductor plays musical recordings and asks the ensemble to identify simple or compound meters by conducting or by tonguing subdivisions with a whisper (see *whisper-tongue* in Glossary).

Students compare and contrast 2/4, 6/8 (3/4, 9/8...) by saying the subdivision and stepping the meter.

Related warm-ups

Following this warm-up:

- Exploring subdivision (warm-up 24)

- Grouping subdivisions of the beat (warm-up 25)

- Working with duple/triple subdivision of steady beat (warm-up 26)

15 Exploring conducting movements

Materials

None

Check for understanding

Ask pertinent questions: Ask students to describe the job of a conductor.

Assess ability: Ask the ensemble to show how a conductor moves to a musical recording.

Experience the concept

Students explore different types of arm movements a conductor might use. They share ideas, copy each other's movements, and describe them.

Student conductors try one movement to synchronize the ensemble into steady beat.

Students find a way to move their arms to organize steady beats into groups of two or three. They share ideas, copy each other's movements, and describe them.

Facilitate and reflect

Why is it important for you to know what a conductor does?

What types of arm movements were the most successful in synchronizing the ensemble?

Apply to ensemble/repertoire

Using steady-beat movement, student conductors lead the ensemble in an unaccented scale.

Student conductors lead the ensemble in accented beat groupings of two or three.

Extend the experience

Students form groups of two. The first partner in each group conducts using beat groupings of two or three beats. The second partner in each group copies, and both partners label with sound (mark the beat with a body part, action, or any sound), accenting the first beat of each group. The second partner identifies the beat grouping. Partners switch roles.

The conductor leads the group by using the actual conducting patterns for beat groupings of two or three. Students compare these to their original patterns.

Related warm-ups

Preceding this warm-up:

- Developing steady beat independence (warm-up 2)
- Applying macrobeat and microbeat knowledge (warm-up 5)
- Understanding the organization of duple meter (warm-up 10)
- Understanding the organization of triple meter (warm-up 11)

Following this warm-up:

- Working with conducting patterns (warm-up 16)

Possible Key Experiences
Describing movement
Moving in nonlocomotor ways
Feeling and expressing steady beat

16 Working with conducting patterns

Materials

"Tsamikos" (CD 2) and "Rebetic Hasápikos" (CD 6)

Other musical recordings with clear meter structure, such as "Gaelic Waltz" (RM 1) and "Kuma Echa" (RM 7)

Check for understanding

Ask pertinent questions: Ask students to tell what they know about conducting patterns.

Assess ability: Ask students to show the conducting patterns they know and say how many beats there are in each.

Experience the concept

Students form groups of two. Partners explore which movements of conducting patterns are always the same, share ideas, copy each other's movements, and describe them.

Conducting a two-beat pattern with both hands, students step or walk the beat and say "down-up" (3-beat = down, out, up; 4-beat = down, in, out, up).

Students form small groups. One student in each group conducts, and the rest of the group moves. Each group picks one way to move for every downbeat and a different way to move for all other beats. Each group determines the meter (the student conductor can use mixed meters).

Facilitate and reflect

What did you learn as a conductor? As a follower?

How will this help you in the ensemble?

Apply to ensemble/repertoire

Various students conduct current repertoire, using creative movement patterns first and then traditional movement patterns. Students compare and contrast.

Individual students watch the conductor conduct the ensemble and make observations as to the style of conducting.

Extend the experience

The conductor uses more difficult meters (for example, mixed or uncommon meters).

Student conductors change tempo and add fermatas while the ensemble performs selections from current repertoire.

Students walk a given beat and conduct in different meters, then add recorded music.

Related warm-ups

Preceding this warm-up:

- Developing steady beat independence (warm-up 2)
- Applying macrobeat and microbeat knowledge (warm-up 5)
- Understanding the organization of duple meter (warm-up 10)
- Understanding the organization of triple meter (warm-up 11)

3

Rhythm

Objective

The objective of this chapter is to have students learn to recognize, understand, and reproduce a variety of rhythm patterns. It is important for an ensemble to be beat-competent in order to provide a strong foundation for rhythmic precision.

Warm-Ups 17–29

17) Performing long and short sounds
18) Using creative rhythmic notation
19) Understanding note division versus note duration
20) Understanding note value relationships
21) Feeling and performing sustained notes
22) Layering rhythm over steady beat
23) Developing rhythmic independence
24) Exploring subdivision
25) Grouping subdivisions of the beat
26) Working with duple/triple subdivision of steady beat
27) Working with uncommon meters through subdivision
28) Feeling even rhythm versus uneven rhythm
29) Feeling swing rhythm versus straight rhythm

Warm-Up Tips

- This process provides real-time assessment (active nonwritten assessment).
- Use a neutral syllable to speak rhythms before using numbers.
- All ideas can be simplified or extended to meet the needs of your ensemble.
- Start where your learners are, not where you want them to be.

17 Performing long and short sounds

Materials

Pencils, pens, and paper

Check for understanding

Ask pertinent questions: Ask students to describe how they can produce long or short sounds.

Assess ability: Ask students to perform long or short sounds by using their voices, body movements, or musical instruments.

Experience the concept

Students explore ways to show the concepts of *long* and *short* through movement. Partners share and copy each other's ideas, describe movements, and share what they've discovered with the whole group.

Students form groups of two. The first partner in a group performs a long or short movement. The second partner copies and interprets it with sound. Partners switch roles.

Facilitate and reflect

What element of music most relates to long and short sounds?

In what ways do the concepts of *long* and *short* feel different through movement?

Apply to ensemble/repertoire

A student conductor shows with body movements when to perform long or short sounds. Ensemble members respond with their own body movements and sounds.

Students locate and identify long and short sounds found in current repertoire.

Extend the experience

Students find a way to represent long and short sounds with art supplies (paper, pencils, crayons, chalk, objects, and so on).

Students find examples of *long* and *short* in note values.

Related warm-ups

Following this warm-up:

- Using creative rhythmic notation (warm-up 18)

- Understanding note division versus note duration (warm-up 19)

- Understanding note value relationships (warm-up 20)

18 Using creative rhythmic notation

Materials

Crayons or pencils

Paper

Check for understanding

Ask pertinent questions: Ask students to define the term *rhythmic notation*.

Assess ability: N/A

Experience the concept

Partners or small groups explore different combinations of long and short movements (see diagram below).

Ensemble members share ideas, copy them, and describe combinations of long and short (longer and shorter) movements.

Each person creates original notation for a long and short pattern. The group shares various notation ideas and interprets with movement and sound.

Facilitate and reflect

How did you choose your symbols for long and short tones?

Look at some traditional rhythmic notation. How do you think traditional notation was created?

Why do we notate (write) music?

Apply to ensemble/repertoire

Ensemble members compare and contrast their original rhythmic notation with traditional rhythmic notation and discuss the similarities and differences.

The ensemble looks at a few musical selections that use modern creative notation and discuss how they would perform these selections. If possible, they listen to a recording of them.

Extend the experience

Using original notation, the ensemble creates a rhythm piece for performance.

Students listen to a recording of a simple instrumental selection, create notation, and compare their notations to the original.

Related warm-ups

Preceding this warm-up:

- Performing long and short sounds (warm-up 17)

Following this warm-up:

- Understanding note value relationships (warm-up 20)

19 Understanding note division versus note duration

Materials

None

Check for understanding

Ask pertinent questions: Ask students to define the terms *division* and *duration.*

Assess ability: Keep a beat and ask the ensemble to pat a division or duration over the beat as directed.

Experience the concept

Students explore ways to keep steady beat with body movements, make sounds lasting more than one beat (duration), and make multiple sounds per beat (division).

One student leads the group with a steady beat, and each group member shows note duration or division through movement. Working in groups of two, one partner in each group leads the beat, while the other partner shows the note duration through movement. Both partners label the movement with sound or movement.

Facilitate and reflect

What is the relationship between division and duration and steady beat?

What repertoire do you know that uses a lot of division or duration?

Apply to ensemble/repertoire

In current repertoire, students find examples of division and duration of steady beat.

Student conductors show warm-up patterns of steady-beat duration or division. The ensemble performs and labels the beat with sound or movement.

One student leads the whole ensemble on steady beat, then uses a neutral syllable to speak a duration or division. The ensemble labels the beat with sound or movement.

Extend the experience

The percussion section keeps a steady beat, the woodwind section plays one duration on a unison pitch, and the brass section plays another length of duration on a harmonizing pitch. Students follow the same steps with beat division.

As the whole choir steps the beat, one group (all women, or all sopranos, or all tenors, depending on the choir's makeup) sings one duration, while the other group (all men, or all altos, or all basses and baritones) sings another. Students follow the same steps with beat division.

Related warm-ups

Preceding this warm-up:

- Developing steady beat independence (warm-up 2)
- Performing long and short sounds (warm-up 17)

Following this warm-up:

- Understanding note value relationships (warm-up 20)
- Layering rhythm over steady beat (warm-up 22)

20 Understanding note value relationships

Materials

None

Check for understanding

Ask pertinent questions: Ask students to explain the values of whole, half, quarter, and eighth notes.

Assess ability: Give students an approximate quarter-note beat and ask them to pat the whole-, half-, and eighth-note values.

Experience the concept

Students explore long, short, longer, and shorter movements. Students then form groups of two. Partners share ideas, copy them, and describe their movements.

Partners in each group of two create four movements and arrange them in order of long, longer, short, and shorter. Partners then find a way to relate each value to each of the other values (for example, *long* = 1/2 of *longer,* and so on). Partners share and try each other's ideas.

Students put ideas into the context of whole, half, quarter, and eighth notes.

Groups of four students create movements for whole, half, quarter, and eighth notes. They perform the movements, starting with one and adding the others one at a time.

Facilitate and reflect

What are the actual values of whole, half, quarter, and eighth notes, and how do they relate to each other?

What does movement have to do with note values (time and space)?

What relationship does steady beat have to note values?

Apply to ensemble/repertoire

Students use note values and scales to create warm-ups. For example, brass instrumentalists play scales on whole notes, woodwind instrumentalists play on half notes, and percussionists keep quarter-note beat. Sopranos in a chorus sing pitch on whole notes, altos sing on half notes, tenors on quarter notes, and basses on eighth notes.

The conductor finds a rhythmic passage from current repertoire that is causing problems for student performers. Students use foot movements to keep the given quarter-note beat (by metronome marking in music). They use neutral syllables to speak the rhythm pattern.

Extend the experience

Groups of students move to different four-note values simultaneously in order to put note relationships into visual mode (one group moves to quarter notes, one group to half notes, and so on.)

Each individual in a group of four students performs whole-, half-, quarter-, and eighth-note values simultaneously.

Each student uses movement to perform two or three note values simultaneously.

Related warm-ups

Preceding this warm-up:

- Performing long and short sounds (warm-up 17)
- Using creative rhythmic notation (warm-up 18)
- Understanding note division versus note duration (warm-up 19)

Following this warm-up:

- Layering rhythm over steady beat (warm-up 22)

21 Feeling and performing sustained notes

Materials

"Hole in the Wall" (RM 4)

Other musical recordings with a moving line over sustained notes, such as "The Sally Gardens" (RM 1)

Check for understanding

Ask pertinent questions: Ask students to describe a sustained note.

Assess ability: Ask students to locate and perform sustained notes in a phrase of current repertoire or in a warm-up.

Experience the concept

In this warm-up, students use either their voices or instruments that produce a long sound (for example, metals, or shaking rattles, and so on).

Students form groups of two. The first partner in a group plays the instrument or sings a sustained pitch. The second partner in the group interprets with movement that equals the length of the sustained pitch. Partners switch roles.

In the same groups of two, the first partner in a group moves his or her fingers along a music stand. The second partner in the group performs a pitch that matches the length of the movement. Partners switch roles.

Facilitate and reflect

What strategies do you use to sustain a pitch?

How can you perform sustained pitches in interesting ways?

Apply to ensemble/repertoire

Students use warm-ups designed to improve sustained pitches and enhance them by having partners create movement to match.

Students find examples of sustained pitches from current repertoire. They brainstorm ways in which movement can help illustrate the playing or singing of sustained pitches and experiment with a variety of ways to perform those pitches, such as crescendo, tone color changes, and tempo.

Extend the experience

Students play a musical recording that has a moving line over sustained pitches. Half of the group creates movements to go with the moving line, while the other half of the group creates movements to show the sustained pitches. Students discuss how the sustained pitches and moving line relate to each other.

Students explore ways to make sustained sounds exciting through movement and pitch. For example, sustained movement can use different pathways or shapes, and sustained pitch can crescendo toward the end.

Related warm-ups

Preceding this warm-up:

- Performing long and short sounds (warm-up 17)
- Understanding note division versus note duration (warm-up 19)

Following this warm-up:

- Feeling rubato (warm-up 66)
- Exploring tone qualities (warm-up 71)
- Understanding the emotional qualities of music (warm-up 73)

Possible Key Experiences
Moving in nonlocomotor ways
Moving in locomotor ways
Expressing rhythm

22 Layering rhythm over steady beat

Materials

"Yankee Doodle" (RM 2)

Other musical recordings that have a strong beat, such as "Road to the Isles" (RM 5) and "Carnivalito" (RM 5)

Check for understanding

Ask pertinent questions: Ask students to describe the relationship between steady beat and rhythm.

Assess ability: Play a musical selection with a strong beat (for example, a march) and signal students when they should use their hands to perform a beat or a rhythm with the music.

Experience the concept

Students step steady beat while exploring whisper-tongued or spoken rhythms.

Small groups step steady beat and use neutral syllables to echo vocal rhythm patterns. Rhythms are given by different student leaders from the group.

A student leader speaks a four-beat pattern many times. The group finds a steady beat by patting silently, then joins in speaking the rhythm.

Facilitate and reflect

How do rhythm and beat interrelate?

As a performer, why is it important to understand the relationship between rhythm and beat?

Apply to ensemble/repertoire

Half of the group pats steady beat, while the other half speaks or whisper-tongues difficult rhythm patterns from current repertoire. Groups switch roles.

Each person pats a beat while speaking his or her own rhythmic parts.

Extend the experience

Students layer voice rhythms over microbeat and macrobeat marked by body movements. They reverse the process, voicing the beat and stepping the rhythm.

Students physically maintain steady beat while performing warm-ups.

Related warm-ups

Preceding this warm-up:

- Developing steady beat independence (warm-up 2)
- Understanding note value relationships (warm-up 20)

Following this warm-up:

- Developing rhythmic independence (warm-up 23)

23 Developing rhythmic independence

Materials

None

Check for understanding

Ask pertinent questions: Ask students to explain what it means to be rhythmically independent.

Assess ability: Divide the ensemble into the desired number of groups and give each group a rhythm that uses specific clapping, patting, snapping, or stamping sounds. Ask all groups to perform their given rhythms and sounds simultaneously.

Experience the concept

Individuals start a steady-beat movement and use a neutral syllable to layer on their own spoken rhythm patterns.

Students form groups of two. The first partner in a group performs steady-beat movement. The second partner copies the same beat and movement. Both partners then use a neutral syllable to layer on their own spoken rhythms (feeling the same beat, but hearing different rhythms simultaneously).

Facilitate and reflect

Why do we need to develop rhythmic independence?

What did you learn from working with polyrhythms (many rhythms performed simultaneously)?

What common elements do various rhythms have?

Apply to ensemble/repertoire

Students suggest ways to perform warm-ups with different rhythms. As half of the group performs a steady-beat movement, the other half performs warm-ups using the suggested rhythms simultaneously.

The conductor finds a portion of a musical selection that has several concurrent rhythms. The ensemble group assigns one specific neutral syllable to each rhythm (for example, *bah* for one rhythm and *be* for another, and so on). The ensemble as a whole unit performs a steady-beat movement. Small groups of students layer on one spoken rhythm after the other until all are going simultaneously. Students discuss how it is possible to keep the rhythms together.

Extend the experience

The ensemble creates a chart (score) of several rhythms. Students represent the chart by using body percussion (patting some part of the body, snapping fingers, and so on) or mimicking environmental sounds.

Students listen to a musical selection that demonstrates polyrhythms. They find a steady underlying microbeat or macrobeat and keep the beat by patting their laps or tapping their feet while using a neutral syllable to chant one of the rhythms.

Related warm-ups

Preceding this warm-up:

- Developing steady beat independence (warm-up 2)

- Understanding note value relationships (warm-up 20)

- Layering rhythm over steady beat (warm-up 22)

Following this warm-up:

- Exploring subdivision (warm-up 24)

- Working together as an ensemble (warm-up 74)

24 Exploring subdivision

Materials

Pencil and paper

"Debka Chag" (CD 1)

Other musical recordings that use beat subdivision, such as "Jessie Polka" (RM 8) and "Irish Washerwoman" (RM 3)

Check for understanding

Ask pertinent questions: Ask students to explain how microbeats can be subdivided.

Assess ability: Ask students to pat macrobeat, step microbeat, and speak or whisper-tongue duple subdivision of microbeat (triple subdivision, if desired).

Experience the concept

Students explore ways to put two, then three, different beats together with movement. They share and copy each other's ideas.

The conductor plays a selection of recorded music. Students explore stepping the microbeat, patting the macrobeat, and marking beat subdivision by speaking neutral syllables. With partners, students copy each other's ideas and describe movements.

To the same musical recording, students explore putting the beats and subdivision in different places (for example, stepping the macrobeat, patting the microbeat, and marking beat subdivision by speaking neutral syllables).

Facilitate and reflect

What is the meter of the musical recording used in the preceding activities? Based on our experiences, how did you determine the meter?

What rhythmic units would the macrobeat, microbeat, and subdivision be in the meter of the recording?

Apply to ensemble/repertoire

The ensemble performs a section of current repertoire. Students discuss which rhythmic units are the macrobeat, the microbeat, and the subdivision.

The ensemble performs a section from current repertoire. Students discuss which rhythmic unit helps them to perform more accurately and why.

Extend the experience

Using different musical recordings, students step the macrobeat and pat the microbeat. They mark beat subdivision by speaking neutral syllables and explore ways to change the beats around.

Students show beat subdivision by using creative notation.

Related warm-ups

Preceding this warm-up:

- Understanding macrobeat and microbeat (warm-up 4)
- Developing rhythmic independence (warm-up 23)

Following this warm-up:

- Grouping subdivisions of the beat (warm-up 25)

25 Grouping subdivisions of the beat

Materials

None

Check for understanding

Ask pertinent questions: Ask students to explain how subdivisions of the beat can be grouped.

Assess ability: Ask students to pat the beat on their laps and divide into groups by using accents.

Experience the concept

Students form groups of two. The first partner in a group starts beat subdivision by making vocal sounds. The second partner explores ways to group the subdivisions by patting or stepping accents. Partners switch roles.

The first partner in each group initiates steady beat. The second partner chants a duple, triple, or quadruple subdivision of the beat.

Facilitate and reflect

What are the relationships of subdivisions to steady beat?

Which was easier or more difficult to start with, beat or subdivisions? Why?

How are subdivisions performed compared to just a steady beat?

Apply to ensemble/repertoire

A student conductor leads steady beat, and the ensemble performs a given subdivision (2, 3, or 4) on a specific pitch or chord.

The ensemble identifies subdivisions in the current repertoire and performs a section of the music, feeling the subdivision internally.

Extend the experience

A student conductor leads steady beat, and the ensemble performs a given subdivision in uncommon meters (5, 7, or 9).

Each student speaks the subdivision in *ch* sounds and groups the subdivisions into 2, 3, or 4 by patting and then by stepping.

Related warm-ups

Preceding this warm-up:

- Developing steady beat independence (warm-up 2)

Following this warm-up:

- Working with duple/triple subdivision of steady beat (warm-up 26)

26 Working with duple/triple subdivision of steady beat

Materials

None

Check for understanding

Ask pertinent questions: Ask students to define the terms *triple subdivision of steady beat* and *duple subdivision of steady beat.*

Assess ability: Ask students to start a steady beat and chant duple or triple subdivision.

Experience the concept

Students form groups of two. The first partner in a group whisper-tongues a steady-beat subdivision. The second partner in the group explores nonlocomotor movement ways to group the subdivisions into twos or threes. The first partner identifies groupings or patterns. Partners switch roles.

Students initiate their own subdivision of steady beat and pat or step accents for duple- or triple-beat groups.

Facilitate and reflect

How did you show duple or triple groups of steady beat?

Why is it important to know beat groupings for performance?

Apply to ensemble/repertoire

The ensemble performs long-tone warm-ups. Half of the ensemble performs a long tone, and the other half performs duple or triple subdivision of beat by making a sound such as a clap.

Students locate difficult sections of current repertoire and perform the sections with part of the ensemble performing subdivision of the beat.

Extend the experience

Partners describe and discuss the organization of beat into twos and threes. They play scales, dividing them into beat groupings of two or three by using accents.

The ensemble steps steady beat and performs a macrobeat grouping of two or three by using an upper body movement.

Related warm-ups

Preceding this warm-up:

- Developing steady beat independence (warm-up 2)

- Understanding simple meter versus compound meter (warm-up 14)

- Grouping subdivisions of the beat (warm-up 25)

27 Working with uncommon meters through subdivision

Materials

"Ivanica" (CD 3)

Other musical recordings that illustrate uncommon meter, such as "Legnala Dana" (CD 6) and "Tsakonikos" (RM 9)

Check for understanding

Ask pertinent questions: Ask students to explain how a meter of 5 (or 7 or 9) could be organized.

Assess ability: Ask students to whisper-tongue a steady subdivision (approximate eighth notes) and organize groups of five by using hand movement on the accents (2+3, 3+2), for example, III II or II III.

Experience the concept

Students form groups of two. The first partner in a group starts subdivision with his or her voice. The second partner in the group organizes into 2 + 3 or 3 + 2, using hand movements to demonstrate accents (microbeat). The first partner identifies the groupings.

The first partner in a group alternates hands to pat uneven microbeat (accents) in 5 (2 + 3 or 3 + 2) or 7 (3 + 2 + 2). The second partner in the group copies and adds vocal subdivision.

Students repeat these two activities and add macrobeat also.

Facilitate and reflect

Which organization of beats was easier to use, uneven microbeat or subdivision? Why?

Which organization would help you perform current repertoire more accurately? Why?

Apply to ensemble/repertoire

The ensemble performs the steady-beat subdivision. Various student conductors lead, organizing the subdivision into uncommon meters.

Students perform uneven microbeat (mark accents with foot movements and even subdivision with alternating hand movements) and use neutral syllables to layer on spoken rhythm.

Extend the experience

Students mark uneven microbeat accents with foot movements, speak the even subdivision, and mark rhythm with alternating hand movements.

Students listen to musical recordings in uncommon meters and add the beat and subdivisions with body movements.

Related warm-ups

Preceding this warm-up:

- Beginning uncommon meter (warm-up 13)
- Exploring subdivision (warm-up 24)
- Grouping subdivisions of the beat (warm-up 25)

28 Feeling even rhythm versus uneven rhythm

Materials

"Alley Cat" (RM 3)

Other musical recordings that illustrate even rhythm and uneven rhythm, such as "Blackberry Quadrille" (RM 2) and "Bechatzar Harabbi" (RM 6)

Check for understanding

Ask pertinent questions: Ask students to describe even rhythm versus uneven rhythm.

Assess ability: Ask students to show various movement examples of even and uneven.

Experience the concept

Students explore marching, walking, jogging, galloping, and skipping. They label each step by speaking the neutral syllable *bah* and share what they notice about the feel of even versus uneven. (Marching, walking, and jogging are even BAH/BAH; galloping and skipping are uneven BAH/bah, BAH/bah.)

Students form groups of two. The first partner in a group moves. The second partner copies the movement and decides whether it is even or uneven. Partners switch roles.

The first partner in a group speaks. The second partner moves. Partners discuss and label movements.

Facilitate and reflect

What did you notice about movements used with even and uneven rhythms?

How would you describe the feel of even versus uneven rhythm?

Apply to ensemble/repertoire

Students label all current repertoire as even or uneven rhythm.

The ensemble performs familiar warm-ups that use even, then uneven, rhythms.

Extend the experience

The conductor plays recordings of various repertoire and has students identify even or uneven rhythms.

One student performs a locomotor movement, and the ensemble plays even or uneven scale tones to match the movement.

Related warm-ups

Preceding this warm-up:

- Layering rhythm over steady beat (warm-up 22)
- Developing rhythmic independence (warm-up 23)

Following this warm-up:

- Feeling swing rhythm versus straight rhythm (warm-up 29)

29 Feeling swing rhythm versus straight rhythm

Materials

Marsalis on Music, a four-part video series for young audiences, written and hosted by Wynton Marsalis (Sony Classical Film and Video, 1995).

"Tipsy" (RM 6) and "Mechol Hagat" (RM 4)

Other musical recordings, such as "Sicilian Tarantella" (RM 6)

Check for understanding

Ask pertinent questions: Ask students to explain how they would perform any given rhythm in a straight versus a swing style.

Assess ability: Draw an eight-beat rhythm on the chalkboard and ask the ensemble to perform the rhythm in straight style, then in swing style.

Experience the concept

Using the eight-beat rhythm patterns given, students walk or march a steady beat and use a neutral syllable to speak the patterns.

Using the same rhythms, students gallop or skip and speak the rhythms again, but match their activity to the feel of the movement. Students discuss the differences between this and the walking/marching experience.

Facilitate and reflect

What is the difference between straight and swing rhythm?

What other terms would apply?

Which style is used for rock? Which is used for jazz? What about swing?

Apply to ensemble/repertoire

Students perform various warm-ups in straight rhythm and then swing rhythm.

Students perform a selection from current repertoire in a style other than the selection's written style and talk about what they've observed.

Extend the experience

Students change between straight and swing rhythms every other measure of given music.

The conductor plays recordings and asks the ensemble to identify examples of straight rhythm versus swing rhythm.

Related warm-ups

Preceding this warm-up:

- Layering rhythm over steady beat (warm-up 22)
- Developing rhythmic independence (warm-up 23)

Pitch and Melody

Objective

The objective of this chapter is to enable musicians to progress from hearing and reproducing pitch patterns to reading and writing melodies.

Warm-Ups 30–41

30) Identifying high and low pitches
31) Matching pitch
32) Improving intonation
33) Using creative melodic notation
34) Locating lines and spaces on the staff
35) Recognizing note direction on the staff
36) Locating pitches on the staff
37) Working with the musical alphabet
38) Improving the flow of note reading
39) Exploring aspects of melody
40) Understanding whole and half steps
41) Recognizing melody versus accompaniment

Warm-Up Tips

- Instrumentalists should sing parts before playing them.
- Sing parts on neutral syllables before using numbers, letters, solfeggio, or words.
- This process provides real-time assessment (active nonwritten assessment).
- All ideas can be simplified or extended to meet the needs of your ensemble.
- Start where your learners are, not where you want them to be.

30 Identifying high and low pitches

Materials

None

Check for understanding

Ask pertinent questions: Ask students to describe the difference between high and low pitch.

Assess ability: Perform a pattern of high and low pitches. Ask students to echo the pattern and stand or sit to represent the high and low pitches in the pattern (a big interval between pitches is easiest to use for this activity).

Experience the concept

Students explore the many ways in which they can move their bodies high and low. They add high and low sounds to match the movements, then share and copy each other's ideas.

Students form groups of two. The first partner in a group shows a movement pattern that uses a combination of high and low pitches. The second partner in the group copies the movement pattern and adds a matching sound. Partners switch roles.

The first partner in a group sings a pattern. The second partner in the group echoes the singing pattern and adds movement. Partners switch roles.

Facilitate and reflect

Which was easier to follow, singing patterns or showing them with movement?

What helped you to identify whether a pitch was high or low?

Recall some of the movements you created to represent high and low pitches and tell why you chose them.

Apply to ensemble/repertoire

Half of the ensemble performs a selection from current repertoire. The other half listens for high and low pitches that stand out in the music and matches them with movement. Partners switch roles.

Students mark the highest and lowest notes in a phrase of printed music, perform that phrase, and listen to the pitches to see if they match the printed note placement.

Extend the experience

Half of the group represents a folksong chord progression using I–V bass notes, and the other half of the group performs a melody of the folksong. Each group creates movement to represent its part.

The groups repeat the same warm-up activity by using I–IV–V bass notes.

Related warm-ups

Following this warm-up:

- Matching pitch (warm-up 31)

- Improving intonation (warm-up 32)

- Using creative melodic notation (warm-up 33)

31 Matching pitch

Materials

None

Check for understanding

Ask pertinent questions: Ask students to tell what it means to match pitch.

Assess ability: Ask each member of the ensemble to start on a different pitch. Then ask the ensemble to come to a unison pitch (octave, if men's voices).

Experience the concept

Ensemble partners explore ways to match pitch with nonlocomotor movements. They share their ideas with the whole group, try out new ideas, and describe how the movement expresses pitch levels.

Students form groups of two. The first partner in a group draws an up-and-down pathway in the air. The second partner in the group copies the pathway and adds vocal sound to match. Both partners synchronize their movement pathways and vocal pitches. Partners switch roles.

The first partner in a group uses a neutral syllable to sing a pitch. The second partner in the group holds a hand up to the level where he or she thinks the pitch is and tries to match the pitch vocally. Partners switch roles.

Facilitate and reflect

What do you need to be able to match pitch?

How does movement help locate and match pitches?

How does movement relate to printed music?

Apply to ensemble/repertoire

In small groups, students begin singing a song such as "Twinkle, Twinkle, Little Star" in different keys and explore ways to end up in the same key.

Using a selection from current repertoire, students follow the melodic line with a finger and move their voices in the approximate pitch direction. Students match up with a partner and listen to the actual pitch movement to see how close the approximate pitches were to the actual pitch.

Extend the experience

Students stand in a grid formation of rows and columns and use a vowel sound to sing a unison/octave pitch. They sing the pitch two times, concentrating the first time on synchronizing pitch within the row and the second time on synchronizing it within the column.

Students try to vocalize a unison/octave pitch by using different vowel sounds to see if the pitch changes. Students then decide which vowel is the most accurate.

Related warm-ups

Preceding this warm-up:

- Identifying high and low pitches (warm-up 30)

Following this warm-up:

- Improving intonation (warm-up 32)

- Using creative melodic notation (warm-up 33)

- Recognizing note direction on the staff (warm-up 35)

Possible Key Experiences

Acting upon movement directions
Moving in nonlocomotor ways
Developing melody

32 Improving intonation

Materials

None

Check for understanding

Ask pertinent questions: Ask students to explain what it means to be in tune with someone else.

Assess ability: Without giving guidelines, ask students to tune with each other (singers perform unison pitches).

Experience the concept

Students explore pitch individually by moving their arms up and down and matching their movement with voice sounds.

Students synchronize their movements with a partner and explore ways to match pitches.

Students form groups of two. The first partner in the group places both hands in front of his or her body. The second partner in the group moves his or her hands from above or below to match the level of the first partner's hands. The first partner adds vocal pitches and the second partner tries to match them. Partners switch roles.

Facilitate and reflect

What causes a pitch to change?

What strategy did you use to determine that the pitches were in tune?

Discuss the differences between vocal and instrumental tuning.

Apply to ensemble/repertoire

A student conductor sings or plays one pitch. The group tunes to the given pitch.

Students find places in current repertoire where the ensemble or sections perform unison pitches or phrases. They experiment with tuning adjustments.

Extend the experience

Two students from each instrumental or vocal section move from a wide variance in pitch to the same pitch. The rest of the students in the sections match their respective two pitches with up-and-down hand movements and indicate when their section's two students are in tune.

Vocal sections tune octaves. Half of the students match pitches at the octave while the other half of the group listens to intonation and makes corrections.

Related warm-ups

Preceding this warm-up:

- Identifying high and low pitches (warm-up 30)

- Matching pitch (warm-up 31)

Following this warm-up:

- Exploring tone qualities (warm-up 71)

33 Using creative melodic notation

Materials

Paper and pencil

Recording of a Gregorian chant

Check for understanding

Ask pertinent questions: Ask students to define the terms *melody* and *notation*.

Assess ability: N/A

Experience the concept

Students use movement to show the up or down direction of notes in a melody. They share their ideas, copy them, and describe their movements with a partner.

Listening to a Gregorian chant (or a similar style of music), students show melodic direction with movements and then with lines drawn on paper with pencil.

Using paper and pencil, partners create their own style of notation for melody. They "read" each other's creative notation by using movement and vocal sounds (approximate melody).

Facilitate and reflect

What are some characteristics of a melody?

What strategies did you use to create your own notation?

How does your notation compare to actual musical notation on a staff?

Apply to ensemble/repertoire

Using movement and creative notation, students illustrate a melody chosen from current literature. Students compare their creative notation of the melody to the original notation and discuss characteristics that are the same and those that are different.

Extend the experience

Students create their own melodies and then use their own symbols to notate. They exchange papers and decode each other's notations by using movement and singing.

Students research how notation came about and what early notation looked like.

Related warm-ups

Preceding this warm-up:

- Identifying high and low pitches (warm-up 30)

Following this warm-up:

- Recognizing note direction on the staff (warm-up 35)

Possible Key Experiences
Moving in nonlocomotor ways
Moving in locomotor ways
Reading music

34 Locating lines and spaces on the staff

Materials

Large roll of masking tape for use in creating a large music staff on the floor (with lines and spaces)

Check for understanding

Ask pertinent questions: Ask students to tell what they know about the music staff.

Assess ability: Ask students to show line notes and space notes on a music staff.

Experience the concept

Students explore ways to place themselves on the lines and spaces of a large music staff created on the floor or ground with tape.

The conductor or a student leader asks students to place themselves on a line or a space of the floor staff. Students extend the experience by placing two parts of their bodies on two different lines or spaces.

Facilitate and reflect

When you were exploring lines and spaces on the staff, what things did you notice?

How will you remember what a line note is? How will you remember what a space note is?

Apply to ensemble/repertoire

Students locate line and space notes written on a staff.

Students find line and space notes in a selection from current repertoire and determine how they are organized in different patterns.

Extend the experience

Students develop strategies to locate line and space notes written on a staff.

The conductor extends this lesson to naming line and space notes on a staff by number (for example, a line note is on the first line, a space note is on the fourth space).

Related warm-ups

Following this warm-up:

- Recognizing note direction on the staff (warm-up 35)

- Locating pitches on the staff (warm-up 36)

Possible Key Experiences
Moving in nonlocomotor ways
Acting upon movement directions
Reading music

35 Recognizing note direction on the staff

Materials

Large roll of masking tape for use in creating a large music staff on the floor and wall (with lines and spaces)

Check for understanding

Ask pertinent questions: Ask students to tell what they know about going up and down on a staff.

Assess ability: Ask students to show up and down on a staff.

Experience the concept

Students create a staff on the floor with tape. They explore ways to go up and down the floor staff, share their ideas, copy each other's ideas, and describe their movements.

Students create a staff on the wall with tape. They move their hands up and down on the wall staff to illustrate directional vocal sounds.

Facilitate and reflect

How can you tell which direction is up on the staff without notes?

How can you *remember* which direction is up on the staff?

Apply to ensemble/repertoire

Students form groups of two. The first partner in a group sings or plays an up-and-down pattern. The second partner in the group moves his or her hands along the staff to match the direction of sounds made by the first partner.

Students find sections from current repertoire in which the note direction is clear. They indicate whether the direction is up or down and use a neutral syllable to sing approximate pitches.

Students choose a short portion from current repertoire. They use a pencil to connect the note heads and determine the melodic direction or pathway. Students then move their hands along that pathway and match each note with pitches. They compare their pitches to the actual sound of the notes.

Extend the experience

Students create their own road map of up-and-down lines and notes on the staff and compare their work.

Students listen to a simple song such as "Twinkle, Twinkle, Little Star" and make approximate up-and-down notations on the staff.

Students identify up-and-down direction in a given written melody.

Related warm-ups

Preceding this warm-up:

- Using creative melodic notation (warm-up 33)

Following this warm-up:

- Locating pitches on the staff (warm-up 36)

36 Locating pitches on the staff

Materials

Large roll of masking tape for use in creating a large music staff on the floor (with lines and spaces)

Check for understanding

Ask pertinent questions: Ask students to talk about how notes are organized on a staff.

Assess ability: Ask students to read a short excerpt of letter note names on the staff (C, B, A, and so on).

Experience the concept

Students use different locomotor movements to explore a variety of pitches on a staff created on the floor with tape.

Student leaders give note names, and other students use a variety of locomotor movements to locate these notes on the floor staff.

Facilitate and reflect

What strategies did you use to locate notes on the staff?

How can you use these strategies when you are reading music?

Apply to ensemble/repertoire

Using pitch names, students practice singing excerpts from current repertoire.

Students find notes on the staff using various clefs (depending on the needs of the ensemble).

Extend the experience

Students create their own melodies and notate on a staff. Others read the notes and perform the music.

Students spell words on the floor staff by jumping on the notes in order. Other students identify the note names.

Related warm-ups

Preceding this warm-up:

- Locating lines and spaces on the staff (warm-up 34)

Following this warm-up:

- Working with the musical alphabet (warm-up 37)

- Understanding whole and half steps (warm-up 40)

37 Working with the musical alphabet

Materials

None

Check for understanding

Ask pertinent questions: Ask students to tell what they know about the musical alphabet.

Assess ability: Ask students to say and show the musical alphabet with hands representing the direction of the notes, beginning with middle C.

Experience the concept

Students explore moving hands up and down, speaking, and then singing the musical alphabet forward (up—a,b,c...) and backward (down—c,b,a...).

Students form groups of two. The first partner in a group puts his or her hands in a starting note position and names a note. The second partner in the group says "up" or "down" and says the name of the next note. Partners follow the same steps as in the first activity, but sing the notes.

A student leader chooses a letter from a visual representation of the musical alphabet. The leader then points to different letters one at a time. The group names each letter and states whether its direction is up or down. Students in the group move their hands in that direction.

Facilitate and reflect

What did you learn from this experience?

What are other ways to work with the musical alphabet?

Apply to ensemble/repertoire

The conductor or a student leader plays a stepwise melody (one pitch after the other, for example *abc,* or *edc*).

Students in the group move their hands in the direction of the notes and say "up" or "down."

The conductor sings or plays a starting note and says "up" or "down." The group names the next pitch and sings or plays that pitch.

Extend the experience

The conductor or a student leader plays a stepwise melody. Students in the group move their hands in the direction of the notes, name whether the direction is up or down, and try to name the note.

The conductor plays a melody that skips pitches (for example, *gec*). The group analyzes and decides how to show skips by using up or down hand movements. The group tries to name the note with a letter.

Related warm-ups

Preceding this warm-up:

- Identifying high and low pitches (warm-up 30)
- Using creative melodic notation (warm-up 33)

Following this warm-up:

- Understanding whole and half steps (warm-up 40)

38 Improving the flow of note reading

Materials

Large roll of masking tape for use in creating a large music staff on the floor (with lines and spaces)

Cards depicting notes on music staff

Staff-lined paper and pencils

Check for understanding

Ask pertinent questions: Ask students to tell what they understand about reading notes on a staff.

Assess ability: Ask students to sight-read a portion of new repertoire (or a simple song, depending on the experience of your group). Then ask students to use a neutral syllable to sing the notes.

Experience the concept

Students form small groups. Each person explores ways to move up and down the staff taped to the floor, landing on lines or spaces and naming the notes. Once each person has had an opportunity to do this, one person names a note, and the person in front of him or her moves to that note on the floor staff. Students repeat this activity until each of them has had an opportunity to both name and move to a note on the floor staff chosen by another. Students work on their note memorization by extending the activity to two, three, and four notes at a time.

A student leader names two, three, four, or five notes in succession, and the rest of the group marks the correct line or space on staff-lined paper with stickers, popcorn, beans, or similar objects. Notes can also be marked with hands or elbows on a staff created on the wall with tape.

Facilitate and reflect

How do you read several notes on a staff at one time as opposed to one at a time?

What ideas do you have for improving music-reading skills?

What does recognizing high and low notes have to do with music reading?

Apply to ensemble/repertoire

Using a new musical selection, each student states the letter names of the notes in the first measure as quickly as possible. Students sing and move their hands in front of their bodies simultaneously with each note. Students follow the same steps with the second measure, perform the first measure again, and follow with the second measure. They continue on as far as needed.

Students sight-read the first four measures without stopping to make corrections. They perform their individual parts together as a warm-up. The ensemble performs the first four measures again. The group discusses how the second reading compares to the first.

Extend the experience

Students mark the trouble spots in a new piece of music after sight-reading. They work in groups on reading the notes.

A student leader names a series of five notes. Students use neutral syllables to speak the notes and then jump on the appropriate lines and spaces of a staff created on the floor with tape. They practice looking ahead at the next note in the series while landing on the previous note on the floor staff.

Related warm-ups

Preceding this warm-up:

- Locating lines and spaces on the staff (warm-up 34)
- Working with the musical alphabet (warm-up 37)

39 Exploring aspects of melody

Materials

A familiar folksong, such as "This Land Is Your Land," by Woody Guthrie

Check for understanding

Ask pertinent questions: Ask students to define the term *melody.*

Assess ability: Ask students to play or sing a melody.

Experience the concept

Using a simple song such as "This Land Is Your Land," students explore ways to represent the melody through movement, such as moving their arms in the direction of the melody or to represent the song's dynamics, patterns, form, and so on. They share and copy each other's ideas and brainstorm the similarities and differences in interpreting melody.

Students draw the pathway of a melody on paper. They sing or play the actual melody while looking at the drawing. Then they compare the actual staff notation and the drawing.

Facilitate and reflect

What are some of the aspects of melody?

Where does melody come from?

What is the easiest aspect of melody to hear?

Apply to ensemble/repertoire

Students perform a melody from current repertoire and brainstorm its characteristics. Students then bring the entire melody alive through movement representing each aspect of the melody—speaking the rhythmic patterns (using neutral syllables), moving their hands up and down to the melody's contour, creating a dance to the form, showing the tension and release through body movement, showing the beginning and end, and so on.

Students apply the above activities to a new melody from current repertoire.

Extend the experience

The ensemble creates and performs a melody that uses two, three, and five tones. Students add variations and movement.

Students compare melodies from different cultures by performing them and discussing how the music affects the dance styles. (Include this extension only if students have an appropriate knowledge base.)

Related warm-ups

Preceding this warm-up:

- Using creative melodic notation (warm-up 33)

Following this warm-up:

- Recognizing melody versus accompaniment (warm-up 41)

40 Understanding whole and half steps

Materials

Paper and pencil

Check for understanding

Ask pertinent questions: Ask students to define whole and half steps.

Assess ability: N/A

Experience the concept

Students explore walking in pathways that represent whole steps and half steps. They share ideas with the whole group, try out new ideas, and describe how the movement expresses whole and half steps.

Partners create pathways by using combinations of whole and half steps. The conductor copies different pathways by playing a scale to match chosen whole and half steps.

The conductor performs a chromatic scale. Students analyze and create pathways to match it (using all half steps).

The conductor performs a whole-tone scale. Students analyze and create pathways to match it (using all whole steps).

Facilitate and reflect

What is the relationship between whole and half steps?

How do whole and half steps sound different?

How does moving the whole and half steps help you with listening?

Apply to ensemble/repertoire

Students find whole- or half-step patterns in current repertoire. They create pathways on the floor or create an illustration of the pathway with paper and pencil. Then they find and travel the major scale pathway.

Extend the experience

Students create pathways to go with minor scales and other modes.

One section of the ensemble plays a melodic phrase from current repertoire as the rest of the ensemble creates a visual or movement pathway for the progression of whole or half steps (keep melody very simple).

Related warm-ups

Preceding this warm-up:

- Identifying high and low pitches (warm-up 30)

- Locating pitches on the staff (warm-up 36)

- Working with the musical alphabet (warm-up 37)

- Exploring aspects of melody (warm-up 39)

Possible Key Experiences

Moving in nonlocomotor ways

Moving in locomotor ways

Moving to music

41 Recognizing melody versus accompaniment

Materials

"Corrido" (RM 5)

Other musical recordings illustrating melody, such as "The Sally Gardens" (RM 1) and "Hole in the Wall" (RM 4)

Check for understanding

Ask pertinent questions: Ask students to explain the difference between melody and accompaniment.

Assess ability: N/A

Experience the concept

The conductor plays a recording of selected music that clearly demonstrates melody and accompaniment (voice and guitar, solo instrument with ensemble). Students explore ways to represent the melody and the accompaniment with arm movement, such as representing the melodic direction or style of each.

Students form groups of two. Partners share ideas and create synchronized movements for both the melody and the accompaniment. Partners share ideas with the entire group. The group can choose specific movements to represent melody and accompaniment.

The conductor repeats the recording. Half of the ensemble shows the melody through movement as the other half shows the accompaniment. Groups repeat the activity and then switch roles.

Facilitate and reflect

How did your movements differ when showing melody compared to your movements showing accompaniment?

Why is it important to know who has the melody?

How will your performance of this music be affected?

Apply to ensemble/repertoire

Each section of the ensemble performs a small portion of a musical selection. The rest of the group decides whether it is melody or accompaniment.

Part of the ensemble performs a portion of current repertoire. The rest of the ensemble keeps a silent steady beat (on the body) or uses other movement to represent the melody or accompaniment.

Extend the experience

The ensemble experiments with student suggestions about ways to bring out the melody. The conductor applies these suggestions to the performance of the selection. The group reflects on the suggestions.

The ensemble tries to play the accompaniment as if it were the melody and discusses the changes that had to be made. The ensemble then discusses the differences in the total effect.

Related warm-ups

Following this warm-up:

- Achieving ensemble balance (warm-up 70)

Harmony

Objective

The objective of this chapter is to provide a basic understanding of simple bass lines and chord progressions. The student should be able to hear and identify I–IV–V progressions or be able to add the correct chord to a musical selection. Understanding harmony will allow both a vertical view of the music and a horizontal view provided by the bass-line progression.

Hearing other parts and an individual's part in the total piece is also an objective. Working with these ideas will allow musicians to hear their own parts as they fit within the complete harmonic structure of any musical piece.

Warm-Ups 42–45

42. Beginning I–V bass notes
43. Beginning I–IV–V bass notes
44. Beginning 4-bar chord progressions
45. Understanding the 12-bar blues

Warm-Up Tips

- This process provides real-time assessment (active nonwritten assessment).
- All ideas can be simplified or extended to meet the needs of your ensembles.
- Start where your learners are, not where you want them to be.

42 Beginning I–V bass notes

Materials

"Irish Washerwoman" chorus (RM 3)

Check for understanding

Ask pertinent questions: Ask students to tell what they know about bass notes.

Assess ability: Sing or play a simple folksong accompanied by I–V bass notes (V is above the I) and ask students to indicate (with eyes closed) when the bass note should change from I to V.

Experience the concept

After becoming aware of the sound of I and V bass notes (above I), students explore ways to represent I–V patterns through upper body movement. They share ideas and copy each other's movements.

Students form groups of two. The first partner in a group sings a simple song using I–V bass notes. The second partner in the group represents I–V bass notes with movement. Partners switch roles.

Facilitate and reflect

How did you know when the bass notes should change?

How did you decide what movements to use?

What did you hear in the melody that indicated a change in bass notes?

Apply to ensemble/repertoire

The ensemble performs a scale warm-up with a drone bass note provided by the bass voices/instrumentalists in the ensemble. Students repeat the scale. Half of the students represent with movement the places where I or V bass notes could be used.

Students perform a selection from current repertoire and have the bass voices/instrumentalists perform only the tonic bass note. They repeat the selection as originally composed and discuss their findings.

Extend the experience

The ensemble listens to musical recordings that illustrate I–V bass notes, and students show the bass progressions through movement.

The conductor gives the ensemble a variety of simple melodies to perform. Students decide what the pattern of I–V bass notes will be and use I and V bass notes to show how the movements would change.

Related warm-ups

Preceding this warm-up:

- Identifying high and low pitches (warm-up 30)

- Exploring aspects of melody (warm-up 39)

- Recognizing melody versus accompaniment (warm-up 41)

Following this warm-up:

- Beginning I–IV–V bass notes (warm-up 43)

Possible Key Experiences

Moving in nonlocomotor ways

Adding harmony

43 Beginning I–IV–V bass notes

Materials

"Yankee Doodle" (RM 2)

Other musical recordings that illustrate I–IV–V bass notes

Check for understanding

Ask pertinent questions: Ask students to tell what they know about bass notes.

Assess ability: Perform I–IV–V bass notes and ask the students to represent the pattern with movements.

Experience the concept

Students explore and locate pitches I–IV–V in a given scale/key and plan ways to represent the three pitches with nonlocomotor movement.

Students form groups of two. The first partner in a group sings a pattern of I–IV–V pitches. The second partner in the group echoes the pattern and represents the pitches with upper body movement. Partners switch roles.

Students choose a simple folksong that uses I–IV–V bass notes. Half of the ensemble performs the song while the other half represents the chord progression with nonlocomotor movement. This activity can also be done in small groups.

Facilitate and reflect

How did you decide what movements to use for each bass note?

What is the difference in distance between I–IV and I–V?

How did you decide what bass notes to use in the song?

Apply to ensemble/repertoire

Student leaders create warm-ups that use scales and appropriate bass notes. Half of the ensemble performs the scale, and the other half represents the bass notes with nonlocomotor movement.

A student conductor uses creative movements to represent the bass notes to be performed by the ensemble. The ensemble decodes which movements are I–IV and which ones are V by observing the relationship between the student conductor's movements.

Students identify I–IV–V progressions in current repertoire.

Extend the experience

Students identify longer bass progressions in more challenging folksongs.

Students decode I–IV–V bass progressions in appropriate musical recordings from related repertoire.

Related warm-ups

Preceding this warm-up:

- Identifying high and low pitches (warm-up 30)
- Beginning I–V bass notes (warm-up 42)

Following this warm-up:

- Beginning 4-bar chord progressions (warm-up 44)

Moving in nonlocomotor ways

Adding harmony

44 Beginning 4-bar chord progressions

Materials

Musical recordings that illustrate the 4-bar chord progression

Check for understanding

Ask pertinent questions: Ask students to define the term *chord progression.*

Assess ability: Perform a 4-bar chord progression by using only I–IV–V bass notes and ask students to represent bass notes with movement.

Experience the concept

In small groups, students explore movements to represent I–IV–V bass notes in 4-bar progressions. They share and copy each other's ideas and describe how the movements represent the bass notes.

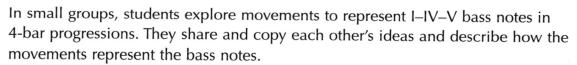

Students form groups of two. The first partner in a group performs a bass pattern. The second partner in the group echoes the bass pattern and represents it with movements. Partners switch roles.

The first partner in a group represents a pattern with movement. The second partner in the group performs the bass pattern. Partners switch roles.

Facilitate and reflect

What is the role of the bass progression?

How does the melody relate to the bass progression?

How does the bass note relate to the chord?

Apply to ensemble/repertoire

Identify bass progressions in current repertoire.

Students create 4-bar chord progressions to accompany warm-ups. Half of the group performs the progressions and the other half represents the progressions with movement.

Extend the experience

Students identify chord progressions in appropriate recordings related to their type of ensemble and the ensemble's current repertoire.

Students add another chord (bass note) to the progressions.

Related warm-ups

Preceding this warm-up:

- Beginning I–V bass notes (warm-up 42)

- Beginning I–IV–V bass notes (warm-up 43)

Following this warm-up:

- Understanding the 12-bar blues (warm-up 45)

Possible Key Experiences

Moving in nonlocomotor ways

Adding harmony

45 Understanding the 12-bar blues

Materials

None

Check for understanding

Ask pertinent questions: Ask students to describe a 12-bar blues bass note progression.

Assess ability: Perform a 12-bar blues bass note progression and ask students to represent the progression with movements for each chord.

Experience the concept

In small groups, students explore how to perform and represent with movement the three 4-bar progressions used in the 12-bar blues (I-I-I-I-IV-IV-I-I-V-I-I-I)*. Students share ideas and try out each other's movements, then decide which movements best represent the chord structure.

Small groups represent one of the 4-bar progressions (or the whole 12-bar progression), with movement only. The ensemble copies the movement and sings the bass notes to match.

Facilitate and reflect

How did movement help you identify the chord progression?

How does a 4-bar chord progression relate to the 12-bar blues chord progression?

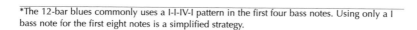

*The 12-bar blues commonly uses a I-I-IV-I pattern in the first four bass notes. Using only a I bass note for the first eight notes is a simplified strategy.

Apply to ensemble/repertoire

A student leader conducts a 4-bar progression using only movement to represent the progressions. The ensemble copies, performs, and identifies which 4-bars of the 12-bar progression the leader conducted.

The ensemble listens to two recorded examples of 12-bar chord progressions. They decide which of the two examples is the 12-bar blues, using movement to identify each chord.

Extend the experience

The ensemble performs 12-bar blues in a variety of keys. Students listen to a recorded musical selection that uses the 12-bar blues chord progression and discuss the similarities and differences in the two selections.

Related warm-ups

Preceding this warm-up:

- Beginning I–V bass notes (warm-up 42)

- Beginning I–IV–V bass notes (warm-up 43)

- Beginning 4-bar chord progressions (warm-up 44)

6

Phrase

Objective

The objective of this chapter is for students to learn to identify, feel, and perform phrases, both symmetrical and asymmetrical. This is based on experiencing and building an understanding of all aspects of phrase, such as beat, rhythm, melodic structure, and expressive qualities (dynamics, timbre, tempo) through movement.

Warm-Ups 46–53

46. Feeling and identifying phrases
47. Working with phrase
48. Understanding the relationship between beat and phrase
49. Driving the phrase rhythmically
50. "Breathing" life into phrase
51. Working with breathing techniques
52. Sculpting phrases
53. Recognizing symmetrical and asymmetrical phrases

Warm-Up Tips

- Many of these ideas can be reinforced through folk dance.
- All ideas can be simplified or extended to meet the needs of your ensembles.
- This process provides real-time assessment.
- Start where your learners are, not where you want them to be.

46 Feeling and identifying phrases

Materials

"Yankee Doodle" (RM 2)

"Tzlil Zugim" (CD 1)

Check for understanding

Ask pertinent questions: Divide the ensemble into pairs or small groups and ask students to discuss what they know about phrases. Ask students to share their thoughts with the whole group.

Assess ability: Play the song "Yankee Doodle." Ask students to walk or to move their hands in a straight line, changing the direction of their movements at the beginning of each new phrase.

Experience the concept

Students explore ways in which they can move both of their hands along the top of a music stand a distance equivalent to the length of a spoken phrase. They share movement ideas, copy each other's ideas, and describe the similarities and differences of their movements.

Facilitate and reflect

What helped you identify the length of the phrase?

What strategies did you use to help make the movement along the music stand and the musical phrases match?

What is the musical importance of feeling phrase?

Apply to ensemble/repertoire

Students use a single neutral syllable to sing "Yankee Doodle." At the same time, they move their hands along the music stand a distance equivalent to the length of the first phrase, pausing at the end of the phrase. They repeat the activity with the rest of the phrases, pausing after each one.

Students identify and mark phrases in current literature. The group performs the marked phrases and discusses the results.

Extend the experience

Students represent with movement the length of phrases in other familiar melodies.

A section of the ensemble performs a selection from current repertoire. The rest of the ensemble members represent phrase length with arm movements. Students compare phrases and discuss any differences.

Related warm-ups

Preceding this warm-up:

- Exploring aspects of melody (warm-up 39)

Following this warm-up:

- Working with phrase (warm-up 47)

Possible Key Experiences

Expressing creativity in movement

Labeling form

47 Working with phrase

Materials

"Al Gemali" (CD 4)

"Bechatzar Harabbi" (RM 6)

Check for understanding

Ask pertinent questions: Ask students to tell what they know about phrase.

Assess ability: Play a recorded musical selection that is related to current repertoire and ask the students to walk or step in place to the phrase length, changing their direction at the beginning of each new phrase.

Experience the concept

Students explore ways to represent phrase length with movement, while singing a song of their choice. They share their ideas with the group. The group tries different movement ideas and compares and contrasts them.

The conductor leads the ensemble in an arm movement to the tune of one of the songs chosen. The ensemble sings and copies the movement.

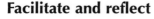

Facilitate and reflect

What did you notice about the differences between student ideas and the conductor's ideas?

How do you find the beginning or end of a phrase?

Apply to ensemble/repertoire

Half of the ensemble represents a phrase with movement. The other half of the group performs a section of current repertoire.

A student conducts the ensemble, using his or her hands to show the length of the phrase (rather than conducting the beat).

Extend the experience

The ensemble divides into four groups. Students in each group represent with upper body movement one of four phrases of recorded music.

Students follow the same steps again, but this time they divide into groups of four. Each student represents one phrase of a recorded musical selection.

Related warm-ups

Preceding this warm-up:

- Feeling and identifying phrases (warm-up 46)

Following this warm-up:

- "Breathing" life into phrase (warm-up 50)

48 Understanding the relationship between beat and phrase

Materials

"Irish Washerwoman" (RM 3)

Check for understanding

Ask pertinent questions: Ask students to define the terms *steady beat* and *phrase*.

Assess ability: Ask students to keep a steady beat in a different place for each phrase.

Experience the concept

With a partner or in small groups, students explore ways to represent the timing of a phrase through movement. They share their ideas, describe their movements, and experience different movements.

Using movement ideas from their exploration, students represent phrases in recorded music. They maintain a steady beat throughout each phrase, changing the placement of the body at the beginning of the phrase.

Facilitate and reflect

How is steady-beat timing used to organize phrases?

What is your new awareness about phrases?

Apply to ensemble/repertoire

After performing a chorale-style warm-up, the conductor asks students to identify phrases and discuss how the organization of the steady beat helped them identify the phrase.

Looking at a new piece of music, each student identifies phrases visually. They share their conclusions and determine how steady beat helped them find and organize phrases.

Extend the experience

Using a familiar folksong such as "Oh, Susannah," students sing and then identify the phrases by creating movements to represent both the steady beat and the length of the phrases.

The ensemble and conductor create a silent piece by using only movement to show the timing with a given length of phrase.

Related warm-ups

Preceding this warm-up:

- Developing steady beat independence (warm-up 2)

- Feeling and identifying phrases (warm-up 46)

Following this warm-up:

- Driving the phrase rhythmically (warm-up 49)

- Sculpting phrases (warm-up 52)

Acting upon movement directions

Expressing rhythm

49 Driving the phrase rhythmically

Materials

None

Check for understanding

Ask pertinent questions: Ask students to define the terms *rhythm* and *phrase* and explain how they are related.

Assess ability: N/A

Experience the concept

Students explore moving their hands smoothly while using neutral syllables to speak rhythms. Phrase length varies.

Students explore putting together four-beat or eight-beat spoken rhythm patterns against body movements that represent beats.

Partners share their rhythm patterns with each other, creating eight-beat patterns.

Students form groups of two. The first partner in the group uses a neutral syllable to speak an eight-beat rhythm pattern, while the second partner in the group smoothly moves his or her hands from one side to the other to show phrase length. Partners switch roles.

Facilitate and reflect

How did you organize your rhythm pattern?

When using ensemble repertoire, what did you notice about how rhythm affected the phrase?

Why is rhythm important to phrase?

Apply to ensemble/repertoire

The conductor or a student speaks the rhythm of the first phrase of a piece of current literature; the ensemble creates an answering phrase with rhythm only, using some of the rhythmic elements included in the first phrase (question and answer).

Ensemble students use a neutral syllable to speak the rhythm of the first phrase of a piece of current literature. They create an answering phrase with rhythm only, using common elements (question and answer).

Extend the experience

Partners create question and answer phrases by using a neutral syllable to speak the rhythms in the phrase while moving a distance equivalent to the length of the phrase.

Listening to representative repertoire, students identify question and answer rhythmic phrases and discuss common and contrasting elements.

Related warm-ups

Preceding this warm-up:

- Developing steady beat independence (warm-up 2)
- Layering rhythm over steady beat (warm-up 22)
- Feeling and identifying phrases (warm-up 46)

Following this warm-up:

- Sculpting phrases (warm-up 52)

Moving in nonlocomotor ways

Labeling form

50 "Breathing" life into phrase

Materials

Any book

Check for understanding

Ask pertinent questions: Ask students to explain how breathing relates to phrasing.

Assess ability: Ask the ensemble to sing a song of its choice, while you observe where the students breathe.

Experience the concept

Each student softly reads an entire paragraph on one breath.

Students read the paragraph again, taking a breath at the beginning of each sentence or phrase. If space allows, students move about the area and change direction with each sentence. If space does not allow, students move their arms and change their movement directions with each sentence.

Facilitate and reflect

How did the text meaning change?

How did you identify and organize the sentences (phrases)?

Apply to ensemble/repertoire

Students sing or play from the beginning of a selection from current repertoire as far as they can sing or play on one breath (they will end at different times). The conductor provides a steady beat throughout.

Students play the same section, breathing at the end of each phrase. If breaths are not taken at the same time, students determine where each phrase ends.

Extend the experience

Student conductors lead the ensemble, indicating the beginning and end of phrases.

Ensemble students listen to various recordings of music and indicate with breaths where phrases are.

Related warm-ups

Preceding this warm-up:

- Feeling and identifying phrases (warm-up 46)

- Working with phrase (warm-up 47)

Following this warm-up:

- Working with breathing techniques (warm-up 51)

- Sculpting phrases (warm-up 52)

51 Working with breathing techniques

Materials

None

Check for understanding

Ask pertinent questions: Ask students to discuss how breathing affects their musical performance.

Assess ability: Ask students to demonstrate their posture and breathing techniques.

Experience the concept

Students explore many different ways to breathe, including using different postures and body positions as space allows. They share, copy, and describe what they discover.

Students explore moving their hands while exhaling; they stop moving their hands when they run out of air. Students extend the breath and movement a little longer each time.

Students repeat the same activity, but this time they sing on random pitches and see how long the pitch can last.

Facilitate and reflect

What are some breathing strategies that will allow longer phrases on one breath?

What positions are best for breathing?

How does breathing apply to string or percussion players?

Apply to ensemble/repertoire

In current repertoire, mark places where a breath should be taken. Half of the group performs a phrase while the other half breathes in on upbeat and out on the remainder of the phrase. Students in the second group move their hands through the space around them while breathing out. Groups switch roles.

Students find a phrase in current repertoire. They sing the phrase first and then play the phrase, if applicable. Students discuss which phrase required the most breath, why it did, and how they can compensate.

Extend the experience

Students listen to a musical selection performed by an ensemble comparable to theirs. They locate phrases and breathe in on upbeats and out during the phrases. Students move their arms or move about the space until the phrase ends.

Students try deep breathing as a relaxation technique before a concert and move their arms with each breath.

Related warm-ups

Preceding this warm-up:

- Working with phrase (warm-up 47)

- "Breathing" life into phrase (warm-up 50)

Following this warm-up:

- Sculpting phrases (warm-up 52)

52 Sculpting phrases

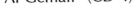

Materials

"Alleluia," by Randall Thompson

"An American Elegy," by Frank Ticheli (vocal or instrumental)

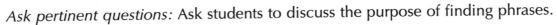

"Hole in the Wall" (RM 4)

"Al Gemali" (CD 4)

Check for understanding

Ask pertinent questions: Ask students to discuss the purpose of finding phrases.

Assess ability: N/A

Experience the concept

Individual students explore the types of movement that might be used to show the tension and release of a phrase. They share ideas with a partner and compare and contrast them.

The ensemble plays the first four phrases of an expressive (or emotional) musical selection, such as Randall Thompson's "Alleluia." Students explore ways to "sculpt" (outline, draw) phrases with the use of hand movements (or by moving other parts of the body).

Students share movements with a partner. They synchronize ways to move together to phrases of "Alleluia" or other selections listed above.

Facilitate and reflect

Why did you choose these specific movements?

How does sculpting or expressing phrases through movement apply to the performance of musical selections?

Apply to ensemble/repertoire

Using arm movements, the ensemble finds ways to sculpt phrases found in current repertoire.

Various students conduct current repertoire, sculpting phrases instead of keeping a steady beat. A second student conductor keeps the beat.

Extend the experience

Students listen to musical recordings that illustrate phrases. They describe the phrases and plan performance according to the sculpted phrase structure.

While the music is playing, students use markers and paper to sculpt phrases of any musical selection. They share and compare ideas.

Related warm-ups

Preceding this warm-up:

- Feeling and identifying phrases (warm-up 46)

- Understanding the relationship between beat and phrase (warm-up 48)

- Driving the phrase rhythmically (warm-up 49)

- "Breathing" life into phrase (warm-up 50)

Following this warm-up:

- Recognizing symmetrical and asymmetrical phrases (warm-up 53)

Moving in nonlocomotor ways

Labeling form

53 Recognizing symmetrical and asymmetrical phrases

Materials

None

Check for understanding

Ask pertinent questions: Ask students to define the terms *symmetrical phrase* and *asymmetrical phrase.*

Assess ability: Ask each person in the ensemble to use arm movements to represent two symmetrical phrases, followed by two asymmetrical phrases.

Experience the concept

With a partner or in small groups, students explore and describe differences between symmetrical and asymmetrical movements.

Students explore ways to move to eight-beat phrases (symmetrical). They share and copy ideas.

Students explore ways to move to 12-beat phrases (symmetrical). They share and copy ideas.

Students explore ways to move to alternating eight- and twelve-beat phrases (asymmetrical).

Facilitate and reflect

What makes phrases asymmetrical?

What is the difference in feel between symmetrical and asymmetrical phrases?

How do you apply your knowledge of symmetrical and asymmetrical phrases to your performance?

Apply to ensemble/repertoire

Students name a selection of current repertoire that uses both symmetrical and asymmetrical phrases. They mark the phrases and play the selection, focusing on the feel of the phrases.

Students find warm-ups that can be changed to asymmetrical phrases.

Extend the experience

Partners perform question and answer phrases with movement; the answer can be the same (symmetrical) or a different (asymmetrical) length from the question.

The ensemble listens to a musical selection that uses both symmetrical and asymmetrical phrases, such as Randall Thompson's "Alleluia." Students represent the length of the phrase with movement.

Related warm-ups

Preceding this warm-up:

- Feeling and identifying phrases (warm-up 46)

- Working with phrase (warm-up 47)

- Understanding the relationship between beat and phrase (warm-up 48)

Following this warm-up:

- Discovering patterns (warm-up 54)

Form

Objective

The objective of this chapter is for students to learn to recognize the basic structure of a musical selection through analyzing, listening, and moving to the music. The understanding of form gives meaning to the performance in its totality.

Warm-Ups 54—59

54. Discovering patterns
55. Exploring ostinato
56. Understanding AB form
57. Understanding rondo form
58. Creating canons
59. Understanding theme and variations

Warm-Up Tips

- Many ideas can be reinforced through folk dance.
- All ideas can be simplified or extended to meet the needs of your ensembles.
- This process is conducive to real-time assessment (active nonwritten assessment).
- Start where your learners are, not where you want them to be.

Possible Key Experiences

Moving in nonlocomotor ways

Moving in sequences to a
common beat

Labeling form

54 Discovering patterns

Materials

None

Check for understanding

Ask pertinent questions: Ask students to tell what they know about patterns.

Assess ability: Show students two hand or body movements and ask them to create a pattern with the movements.

Experience the concept

Students explore and create their own movement patterns. They share and copy each other's ideas, describing similarities and differences in patterns.

Using movement patterns created above, students add sounds to each movement pattern and perform the pattern.

Students find a pattern in the room and represent the pattern with movement.

Facilitate and reflect

What are the characteristics of a pattern?

What strategies did you use to create and represent the patterns?

What other curricular areas use patterns?

Apply to ensemble/repertoire

Using a piece from current repertoire, students find musical patterns (this could be rhythm, melody, harmony, or form). They share their ideas and describe how they identified the patterns. Students then create movement to represent each pattern.

Students organize current warm-ups in patterns. Examples:

- Performing a scale up one octave, down one octave, and up one octave.

- Performing arpeggios in rhythm patterns.

- Performing a scale with one loud, one soft, one loud, one soft.

Extend the experience

Students create shape patterns on paper with pencil and represent the patterns through movement.

One student creates a pattern with movement, and a partner copies, then describes, the movement, telling what it is about the movement that makes it a pattern.

Related warm-ups

Preceding this warm-up:

- Exploring aspects of melody (warm-up 39)

- Beginning I–IV–V bass notes (warm-up 43)

- Working with conducting patterns (warm-up 16)

Following this warm-up:

- Exploring ostinato (warm-up 55)

Possible Key Experiences

Expressing creativity in movement

Labeling form

55 Exploring ostinato

Materials

None

Check for understanding

Ask pertinent questions: Ask students to define the term *ostinato.*

Assess ability: Ask students to create an ostinato to go with a simple folksong (rhythmic or melodic).

Experience the concept

Students create an ostinato to go with a simple round such as "Row, Row, Row, Your Boat" or "Frère Jacques" and represent it with movement. Half of the students sing the ostinato while the other half represents it with movement.

Taking the same song used above, students add a sound or vocal pitch to each movement representing the ostinato. They perform the ostinato again and represent it with movement and sounds.

Facilitate and reflect

What is the purpose of an ostinato?

What strategies did you use to create an ostinato?

Apply to ensemble/repertoire

Students create ostinato patterns (for example, scales) to accompany warm-ups.

Students create movement patterns to represent ostinatos in current repertoire.

Extend the experience

The conductor adds ostinato patterns to musical selections composed by Passacaglia and Chaconne, if appropriate for his or her ensemble.

Students create ostinatos that are performed simultaneously (rhythmic, melodic).

Related warm-ups

Preceding this warm-up:

- Discovering patterns (warm-up 54)

Possible Key Experiences

Moving in nonlocomotor ways

Moving in locomotor ways

Describing movement

Labeling form

56 Understanding AB form

Materials

"D'Hammerschmieds'sell'n (RM 7)

Check for understanding

Ask pertinent questions: Ask students to tell what they know about form.

Assess ability: Ask students to use movement to represent an AB pattern or to perform an AB pattern of music.

Experience the concept

Students explore ways to move while seated. They share and copy each other's ideas. Students explore ways to move around their chairs. They share and copy each other's ideas.

During the A section of a recorded selection, students move while seated. During the B section, students move around the chairs.

Students form groups of two. The first partner in a group plans a way to represent the musical selection with movement and describes the plan to the second person in the group, who performs the movement. Partners switch roles, but the second partner plans movements that contrast with those of the first partner. Partners add sounds to both sets of contrasting movements to create a new sound and movement pattern for the A and B sections.

Facilitate and reflect

What in the musical selection created the differences in the A and B sections?

What other forms could be created with only two sections of music (AAB, ABA, ABB)?

What helps you identify the form of the music?

What is important about identifying form?

Apply to ensemble/repertoire

Students perform current literature that uses AB form and brainstorm differences between the A and B sections.

Student conductors lead the group with movements chosen to match the A and B sections of a current piece of music. The group performs the A section, switching to the B section when the movement changes.

The conductor rearranges current literature into different forms chosen by students. Students perform the selections and discuss them.

Extend the experience

Students create movements to demonstrate various ways of using A and B sections (AAB, ABB, ABA).

The conductor plays a recording that uses AAABBB form.

The conductor plays a recording that uses ABB form.

Related warm-ups

Preceding this warm-up:

- Feeling and identifying phrases (warm-up 46)

Following this warm-up:

- Understanding rondo form (warm-up 57)

Possible Key Experiences

Moving in nonlocomotor ways

Moving in locomotor ways

Labeling form

57 Understanding rondo form

Materials

None

Check for understanding

Ask pertinent questions: Ask students to define the term *rondo.*

Assess ability: Ask students to perform two selections of music, one with AB form and one with rondo form. Ask students to identify which selection is rondo form.

Experience the concept

Using nonlocomotor and locomotor movements, students explore ways to create short, contrasting sections. For example, the movements in one section could be *heel, step, heel, step,* and movements in another section could be *pat, clap, clap, clap.* Students share their ideas with the whole group.

Using ideas from their exploration, the ensemble creates movement for the A section.

The ensemble divides into smaller groups. Each group uses movement to create B, C, and D sections.

Students perform the movement rondo. The whole ensemble performs the A section. The small groups perform the B, C, and D sections.

Facilitate and reflect

What are the characteristics of a rondo?

How does rondo represent the concept of *same* and *different?*

Apply to ensemble/repertoire

Students play a selection from current repertoire that uses rondo form. They indicate where the contrasting sections begin and end.

The ensemble listens to selections for choir, band, and orchestra that use rondo form. Students identify the form and analyze sections that are different.

Extend the experience

The ensemble listens to recordings and identifies rondo form or a variation of rondo form.

In small groups, students create rondo form visually through the use of shapes, colors, and so on.

Students are given the A section. They then improvise contrasting sections.

Related warm-ups

Preceding this warm-up:

- Feeling and identifying phrases (warm-up 46)
- Understanding AB form (warm-up 56)

Following this warm-up:

- Understanding theme and variations (warm-up 59)

Possible Key Experiences

Moving in nonlocomotor ways

Moving in locomotor ways

Adding harmony

58 Creating canons

Materials

None

Check for understanding

Ask pertinent questions: Ask students to define the term *canon.*

Assess ability: Divide the ensemble into four groups. Ask groups to sing "Row, Row, Row Your Boat" in a four-part canon.

Experience the concept

Students explore various ways to show four steady-beat nonlocomotor or locomotor movements in which all four movements use up the same amount of time.

Students form groups of two. The first partner in the group leads four steady-beat movements, changing at the end of the last beat as the second partner in the group begins his or her four-beat movement.

Using the song "Row, Row, Row Your Boat," the ensemble chooses a four-beat movement for each phrase of the song (for example, four pats, four snaps, four claps, four stamps). Students perform the song with the movements in a two-part canon, beginning with the movements.

Facilitate and reflect

Why is a canon challenging?

What were your strategies in performing a canon successfully?

Apply to ensemble/repertoire

Students create movements to accompany or represent the canons in selections from current literature.

The ensemble analyzes how the canons in current literature are used (for example, in different families of the instruments, with different dynamics, or in different tempi).

Extend the experience

In groups of four, students perform a four-beat movement canon.

With partners, students use sequenced movements instead of single movements for the first four beats (for example, head-shoulders, instead of head-head). As the students are learning sequences in unison, it helps to use the SAY & DO process (see Glossary).

Students use environmental sounds found in the room, or unpitched percussion instruments, to perform canons.

Related warm-ups

Preceding this warm-up:

- Developing steady beat independence (warm-up 2)

- Performing entrances in time (warm-up 9)

- Feeling and identifying phrases (warm-up 46)

Possible key experiences

Moving in locomotor ways

Describing movement

Labeling form

59 Understanding theme and variations

Materials

"Variations on Twinkle, Twinkle, Little Star," by Mozart (The Children's Group, 1997)

Check for understanding

Ask pertinent questions: Ask students to define the terms *theme* and *variation form.*

Assess ability: Ask students to use their voices or instruments to create variations on "Twinkle, Twinkle, Little Star."

Experience the concept

Students explore ways to move about the space. They choose one movement and create ways to vary that movement. For example, if the chosen movement is to *walk,* each student varies his or her body position, speed, intensity, smoothness, and so on. Students share their variations with the group. They copy each other's ideas and describe how the movements varied.

Students sing "Twinkle, Twinkle, Little Star" as it is written and suggest variations. They perform the song in different ways. Students then create movements to go with the original song, changing the movements to match the song variations.

Facilitate and reflect

What are some similarities between the theme and the variations?

What are some ways to vary movement and music?

What are some examples of theme and variation in the room? Outside the room? With instruments?

Apply to ensemble/repertoire

The conductor and students together create variations on current warm-ups to make them more interesting. They use different variations for each repetition.

Students find the theme in a selection from current repertoire. They locate where each variation begins (or find a way to vary the theme) and then represent the theme and variations with movements.

Extend the experience

Students bring in examples of music they listen to at home and locate theme and variations in the music.

Students compare theme and variations to other areas of study to determine if any apply.

Related warm-ups

Preceding this warm-up:

- Exploring ostinato (warm-up 55)
- Understanding rondo form (warm-up 57)

8

Expressive Qualities

Objective

The objective of this chapter is to allow performers to learn how to recreate an aesthetic interpretation of a variety of musical selections. They do this by using movement to explore some of the expressive elements of music, such as tempo, dynamics, flow, articulation, and tonality. These elements are important for the final performance and add depth to the music.

Warm-Ups 60–75

60. Working with *loud* and *soft*
61. Understanding dynamics
62. Exploring and understanding tempo makings
63. Understanding accelerando and ritardando
64. Strategies for increasing tempo
65. Strategies for decreasing tempo
66. Feeling rubato
67. Improving instrumental articulation
68. Improving vocal articulation
69. Understanding staccato and legato
70. Achieving ensemble balance
71. Exploring tone qualities
72. Reacting to major and minor tonalities
73. Understanding the emotional qualities of music
74. Working together as an ensemble
75. Exploring vocal shapes and sounds

Warm-Up Tips

- This process is conducive to real-time assessment (active nonwritten assessment).
- All ideas can be simplified or extended to meet the needs of your ensemble.
- Start where your students are, not where you want them to be.

60 Working with *loud* and *soft*

Materials

"In the Hall of the Mountain King," by Edward Grieg

Other musical recordings that show dynamics

Check for understanding

Ask pertinent questions: Ask students to talk about how they know when to
perform loudly or softly.

Assess ability: Ask students to react through movement or performance to
conducting cues for a given loud or soft pitch or a loud or soft section of music.

Experience the concept

Students explore ways to communicate the concepts of *loud* and *soft* to a group.

Students form groups of two. The first partner in the group uses movement to
represent the concepts of *loud* and *soft.* The second partner in the group makes
the same movements, then represents loud and soft sounds vocally or with body
percussion. Partners switch roles.

The first partner in a group represents loud and soft sounds vocally or with body
percussion. The second partner in the group conducts what he or she heard.

Facilitate and reflect

What types of movement indicated the concepts of *loud* and *soft?*

How does representing loud and soft sounds through movement affect your
performance in the ensemble?

Apply to ensemble/repertoire

A student conductor conducts a musical selection from current repertoire and creates movements to indicate loud and soft parts.

The conductor conducts the same portion of music, creating movements to indicate loud and soft parts. The group compares and contrasts the conducting movements.

Extend the experience

Student conductors vary the conducting in the above activities by creating movements to indicate getting louder, getting softer, and so on.

Students listen to a musical recording and explore ways to move as the music gets continually louder. They discuss the techniques used by the composer to create louder music.

Related warm-ups

Following this warm-up:

- Understanding dynamics (warm-up 61)
- Achieving ensemble balance (warm-up 70)

61 Understanding dynamics

Materials

Musical recordings that show contrasting dynamics

Check for understanding

Ask pertinent questions: Ask students to define the term *dynamics* as it relates to music.

Assess ability: Ask students to perform a short piece of music and add dynamics.

Experience the concept

Students explore ways to show dynamics through movement. They share and copy each other's ideas and describe how the movements represent dynamics.

The ensemble listens to a musical recording that clearly illustrates the concepts of *loud* and *soft,* then adds movement to show dynamics (for example, showing dynamics through conducting).

The ensemble listens to a musical recording that illustrates crescendo (getting louder) and decrescendo (getting softer) and shows these changes through movement.

Students use pencil and paper to create a visual illustration of the concepts *loud, soft, crescendo,* and *decrescendo.*

Facilitate and reflect

How do you produce loud or soft sounds with your voice? How do you produce them with your instruments?

Why are the concepts of *loud* and *soft* important to performing music?

What problems arise when performing crescendo and decrescendo?

Apply to ensemble/repertoire

The conductor finds dynamic markings in selections from current repertoire and concentrates on those sections, using ideas from students to improve dynamics.

Students experiment with varieties of loud and soft sounds (*pp, mp, p, f, mf, ff*) while playing scales or singing warm-ups (for example, scales or arpeggios) and discuss how their voices or instruments achieve these gradations of loud and soft.

Extend the experience

Students explore other ways to produce loud and soft sounds, such as by layering parts.

Students create movements to demonstrate varieties (gradations) of loud and soft sounds. Students perform the movements and have a partner first copy the movements and then assign them a symbol such as *f, mf, p,* or *mp.*

Related warm-ups

Preceding this warm-up:

- Working with *loud* and *soft* (warm-up 60)

Following this warm-up:

- Understanding the emotional qualities of music (warm-up 73)

62 Exploring and understanding tempo markings

Materials

"Hora Hassidit" (RM 5)

Other musical recordings that illustrate different tempos, such as "Ersko Kolo" (RM 4) and "Soultana" (CD 2)

Check for understanding

Ask pertinent questions: Ask students to define the term *tempo* and give examples of tempo markings.

Assess ability: Ask students to use movement to represent an andante tempo and a presto tempo.

Experience the concept

Students use locomotor and nonlocomotor movement to explore the tempos *slow* and *fast.* They compare and contrast their movements.

Students use correct musical terms to label degrees of slow and fast.

Using tempo markings from selections in current repertoire, students conduct in the appropriate tempo.

Facilitate and reflect

What do tempo markings communicate?

When a piece is marked andante with no specific metronome marking, how do you determine the tempo?

Apply to ensemble/repertoire

The ensemble plays a selection from current repertoire that uses many different tempos. Students compare degrees of tempo (for example, degrees of *slow* and *fast*).

Student leaders conduct patterns, and the group determines the tempo marking.

Extend the experience

After listening to a musical recording, the ensemble determines the tempos used.

The ensemble plays a portion of current repertoire and determines whether tempo markings seem appropriate to the style of the piece.

Related warm-ups

Preceding this warm-up:

- Developing steady beat independence (warm-up 2)

Following this warm-up:

- Understanding accelerando and ritardando (warm-up 63)

- Strategies for increasing tempo (warm-up 64)

- Strategies for decreasing tempo (warm-up 65)

Possible Key Experiences

Moving in locomotor ways

Moving in nonlocomotor ways

Describing movement

Recognizing the expressive
qualities of tempo and dynamics

63 Understanding accelerando and ritardando

Materials

Musical recordings that demonstrate accelerando and ritardando

Check for understanding

Ask pertinent questions: Ask students to define the terms *accelerando* and *ritardando.*

Assess ability: Ask students to represent accelerando and ritardando through movement.

Experience the concept

With partners or in small groups, students explore fast or slow ways to move in personal space or about the space. They share and copy each other's ideas and describe how their movements show the concepts of *fast* or *slow.*

With partners or in small groups, students explore ways to represent *slow to fast* and *fast to slow* with movement. They share ideas and describe how their movements showed the ideas of *slow to fast* or *fast to slow.*

Students listen to a musical selection that illustrates accelerando and ritardando. They create a pattern of movement and perform with the music.

Facilitate and reflect

What problems did you face when performing accelerando and ritardando?

What strategies can we use to accelerate or slow down (ritard) evenly?

Apply to ensemble/repertoire

Students locate spots where ritardando or accelerando are marked in selections from current repertoire. Half of the group plays the selection, while the other half of the group performs simple movements to represent accelerando and ritardando. Groups switch roles. Students discuss their success in terms of speeding up or slowing down.

The entire ensemble performs the selection used in the above activity without slowing down or speeding up, even when the music is marked ritardando or accelerando. Students discuss the differences in effect.

Extend the experience

During warm-ups or as they practice selections from current repertoire, students experiment with speeding up and slowing down when doing so is not appropriate. They discuss how to maintain a steady beat.

Related warm-ups

Preceding this warm-up:

- Exploring and understanding tempo markings (warm-up 62)

Following this warm-up:

- Strategies for increasing tempo (warm-up 64)

- Strategies for decreasing tempo (warm-up 65)

- Feeling rubato (warm-up 66)

64 Strategies for increasing tempo

Materials

None

Check for understanding

Ask pertinent questions: Ask students to tell what they know about playing or singing a musical selection more quickly.

Assess ability: Play a recording with a clear accelerando and ask students to pat a steady beat with the music, increasing the tempo along with the recording.

Experience the concept

Students in the ensemble explore their own steady-beat movements, then find ways to increase the tempo. They share and compare each other's ideas.

Students form groups of two. The first partner in a group keeps a steady beat, and the second partner in the group copies it. Then the first partner accelerates the beat. Partners switch roles.

The first partner in a group sings or chants a song or rhyme. The second partner in the group keeps a steady beat or conducts, then accelerates the beat. The first partner follows.

Facilitate and reflect

What challenges did you face as leaders when you tried to accelerate? What challenges did you face as followers?

What strategies can you use to accelerate more gradually?

Apply to ensemble/repertoire

The ensemble identifies sections of acceleration in various selections from current literature. Students discuss the similarities and differences found in each selection.

A student conductor conducts various warm-ups that use acceleration.

Extend the experience

The ensemble responds to conducted acceleration when it is not necessarily marked in the music.

The ensemble sight-reads new literature with a student conductor and responds to portions of music that are accelerated.

Related warm-ups

Preceding this warm-up:

- Developing steady beat independence (warm-up 2)

- Understanding accelerando and ritardando (warm-up 63)

Following this warm-up:

- Feeling rubato (warm-up 66)

Possible Key Experiences

Moving in nonlocomotor ways

Moving in locomotor ways

Feeling and expressing steady beat

Recognizing the expressive
qualities of tempo and dynamics

65 Strategies for decreasing tempo

Materials

Musical recordings that demonstrate ritardando

Check for understanding

Ask pertinent questions: Ask students to tell what they know about slowing down
in a musical selection.

Assess ability: Play a musical recording and ask students to raise their hands when
they hear any portion of the music that slows down (ritardando).

Experience the concept

Students form groups of two to explore ways to lead steady beat and slow the beat
gradually.

The first partner in a group keeps a steady beat as the second partner in the group
follows. The first partner in the group expresses ritardando with movements, and
the second partner follows. Partners switch roles.

Facilitate and reflect

When or why would music get slower or faster?

Which type of ritardando was easier to follow, visual or verbal?

What challenges did you face as leaders when you tried to slow down? What
challenges did you face as followers?

Apply to ensemble/repertoire

The ensemble identifies selections from current repertoire that have sections of ritardando.

Student conductors lead these selections.

Extend the experience

The ensemble responds to conducting ritardandos when none are marked in the music.

The ensemble sight-reads new pieces of repertoire that use ritardando.

Related warm-ups

Preceding this warm-up:

*   Developing steady beat independence (warm-up 2)

*   Understanding accelerando and ritardando (warm-up 63)

Following this warm-up:

*   Feeling rubato (warm-up 66)

66 Feeling rubato

Materials

Musical recordings that demonstrate rubato

Check for understanding

Ask pertinent questions: Ask students to tell what they know about rubato.

Assess ability: N/A

Experience the concept

Students explore nonlocomotor movements that use both accelerando and ritardando and share their ideas with each other.

Students explore accelerando and ritardando by creating their own conducting patterns.

Student conductors lead the ensemble in warm-ups that use accelerando and ritardando.

Student conductors lead the ensemble and use rubato in given sections.

Facilitate and reflect

When or why would composers use rubato in their compositions?

What is difficult about following the conductor in rubato sections of music?

How are ritardando or accelerando related to rubato?

Apply to ensemble/repertoire

The ensemble identifies sections of current repertoire where rubato is used even when it is not marked.

Students identify sections in new repertoire where rubato might be appropriate. Student conductors conduct those areas, and the rest of the group decides if the rubato is appropriate.

Extend the experience

Students listen to representative musical recordings and identify sections where rubato is used. Students then discuss why rubato is used in that particular section.

The conductor leads the ensemble in warm-ups and uses different forms of rubato while focusing on the ensemble's responses.

Related warm-ups

Preceding this warm-up:

- Understanding accelerando and ritardando (warm-up 63)
- Strategies for increasing tempo (warm-up 64)
- Strategies for decreasing tempo (warm-up 65)

Following this warm-up:

- Understanding the emotional qualities of music (warm-up 73)

67 Improving instrumental articulation

Materials

None

Check for understanding

Ask pertinent questions: Ask students to define the term *articulation.*

Assess ability: Ask students to play a concert B-flat scale that uses short and
separated articulation.

Experience the concept

Students explore ways to make short movements and sounds followed by long
movements and sounds. They share and copy each other's ideas and describe
the similarities and differences in their movements.

Individual students articulate a variety of short and long sounds with their
respective instruments. They share and copy each other's ideas and describe
the differences and similarities.

Facilitate and reflect

What are some physical aspects of creating short and separated (staccato) sounds
or smooth and connected (legato) sounds with your instrument?

What kinds of music might use staccato articulation? What kinds might use legato
articulation?

Apply to ensemble/repertoire

Students apply staccato and legato articulation to various warm-ups.

Students isolate and play problem areas and use different articulations.

Extend the experience

Students create their own warm-ups by using combinations of staccato and legato articulations. They make a notebook of warm-ups for the ensemble.

The ensemble listens to various instruments in the percussion section and determines which have the ability to play staccato and which have the ability to play legato. Students use combinations of these instruments in warm-ups.

Related warm-ups

Preceding this warm-up:

- Working with *loud* and *soft* (warm-up 60)

Following this warm-up:

- Understanding staccato and legato (warm-up 69)

68 Improving vocal articulation

Materials

A variety of choral and other vocal musical recordings

Check for understanding

Ask pertinent questions: Ask students to define the term *vocal articulation.*

Assess ability: Ask students to sing a clearly marked musical selection and use correct articulation.

Experience the concept

Students form groups of two. Partners explore body movements that could represent the beginning, middle, and end of a single word and share these movements with the whole group.

The first partner in a group shows movements to represent the beginning, middle, and end of a word. The second partner copies the movements and sings the word on any pitch.

Partners follow these same steps, but this time they extend the length of the word by drawing out the vowel sound. Partners switch roles.

Facilitate and reflect

Why is articulation important to vocal music?

What is the difference in articulation between vowel and consonant sounds?

Apply to ensemble/repertoire

Students find sections of current repertoire that are difficult to articulate and isolate specific words. They use movements created in the "Experience the Concept" section of this warm-up to "sing" each word.

The conductor asks students to locate words in a new piece of music that might prove to be hard to articulate. Students work on these words in small groups before singing as a total group.

Extend the experience

Students listen to a variety of live or recorded choral selections performed by various ensembles. They analyze the articulation and critique the groups. Students take field trips to concerts of quality choral groups and discuss each group's articulation.

Students read passages from poetry or literature, focusing on articulation.

Related warm-ups

Preceding this warm-up:

- Starting and stopping together (warm-up 1)

69 Understanding staccato and legato

Materials

None

Check for understanding

Ask pertinent questions: Ask students to define the terms *staccato* and *legato*.

Assess ability: Ask students to perform a familiar warm-up using staccato, then legato.

Experience the concept

Students explore ways to move smoothly and connected, then short and separated. They share and copy each other's ideas and describe their movements.

Students form groups of two. The first partner in a group conducts a musical selection. The second partner in the group makes staccato or legato movements to the conducted piece. Partners switch roles.

The first partner performs a musical selection. The second partner conducts or matches with movement what he or she hears. Partners switch roles.

Facilitate and reflect

How did you know when to perform staccato? How did you know when to perform legato?

What types of music use staccato? What types use legato? What types use both? Why?

How do you perform staccato? How do you perform legato?

Apply to ensemble/repertoire

Using a selection from current repertoire, student conductors use movement to indicate staccato or legato. The ensemble then performs the selection.

The ensemble performs warm-ups using alternating staccato or legato articulation.

Extend the experience

The conductor asks students to identify staccato or legato in a musical recording.

Students try different tone qualities by using staccato or legato articulation. They extend this activity to other articulations.

Related warm-ups

Preceding this warm-up:

- Performing long and short sounds (warm-up 17)

- Improving instrumental articulation (warm-up 67)

- Improving vocal articulation (warm-up 68)

Following this warm-up:

- Understanding the emotional qualities of music (warm-up 73)

70 Achieving ensemble balance

Materials

Musical recordings that show a balance of melody over accompaniment

Check for understanding

Ask pertinent questions: Ask students to define the term *ensemble balance.*

Assess ability: Ask the ensemble to perform part of a selection from current repertoire without any coaching from you. Then ask them to tell what they noticed about balance.

Experience the concept

Students stand in front of their chairs and step steady beat. They explore differences in dynamic levels and types of stepping sounds and discuss which ones were the most noticeable.

Students use hands, feet, pencils, and so on to keep a steady beat. They discuss how sounds are different, which sounds are dominating, and why this is so.

Facilitate and reflect

Why is balance important to ensemble performance?

What parts of the music should stand out the most?

What elements lead to one part dominating another part?

What are ways to change and improve the balance?

Apply to ensemble/repertoire

The ensemble performs the same selection the conductor used to assess their ability and listens for balance. Students discuss what they noticed.

The ensemble performs the some selection, but various instrumental or choral sections vary their dynamics. Students decide which part should dominate and why.

Extend the experience

The group listens to other live or recorded ensembles and assesses each group's balance.

As the ensemble performs music, the conductor experiments with student suggestions about affecting balance.

Related warm-ups

Preceding this warm-up:

- Recognizing melody versus accompaniment (warm-up 41)
- Working with *loud* and *soft* (warm-up 60)

Following this warm-up:

- Working together as an ensemble (warm-up 74)

71 Exploring tone qualities

Materials

Musical recordings that illustrate a variety of tone colors

Check for understanding

Ask pertinent questions: Ask students to define the terms *tone quality* and *timbre*.

Assess ability: Ask students to perform one pitch by using a variety of tone qualities.

Experience the concept

Students explore a variety of vocal pitches, mouth sounds, or body sounds, and match the sounds with movements. They share and copy their ideas and describe the movements.

Using instruments (in sectionals) students do the activity described above. Students then create a "tone bank" of sounds to pull from when performing.

Students match an instrument sound with a vocal sound and discuss their similarities and differences.

Facilitate and reflect

How can you describe the quality of some of the pitches produced by the voice?

Why is tone quality important to performance?

Apply to ensemble/repertoire

Each section of an ensemble chooses a specific tone quality and performs it. The group describes each section's performance.

The entire ensemble experiments with group tone qualities and labels them for further use.

Students choose current repertoire where tone quality is especially important and perform it by using different tone qualities. Students then choose which tone quality seems most appropriate for the musical selection and explain why.

Extend the experience

The conductor has students listen to various recordings that are relevant to the conductor's ensemble. The conductor then asks students to compare and discuss tone qualities and indicate how and why they were used.

Students listen to various recordings and discuss any differences in tone quality.

Related warm-ups

Preceding this warm-up:

- Improving intonation (warm-up 32)

Following this warm-up:

- Achieving ensemble balance (warm-up 70)

72 Reacting to major and minor tonalities

Materials

Musical recordings in major and minor keys, such as Gustav Mahler's Symphony no. 1, third movement

Check for understanding

Ask pertinent questions: Ask students to discuss the differences in sound between major and minor tonalities.

Assess ability: Play recordings in both major and minor tonalities. Ask students to identify the mood of each piece and represent it with movement.

Experience the concept

Students form groups of two. Partners explore ways to express various emotions with facial expressions. They share and identify the emotions and discuss what it was about the expression that relayed the emotion.

Partners find ways to express emotions through arm or whole body movements. They share and compare their ideas and describe the movements used.

Students listen for differences in tonalities in a musical recording. They discuss these differences and the emotions or moods of each tonality and then represent them with movements.

Facilitate and reflect

What are the musical differences between major and minor tonalities?

What are some of the emotions you felt with the major tonality? What did you feel with the minor tonality?

How does feeling emotions relate to your performance as an ensemble?

Apply to ensemble/repertoire

The conductor and members of the ensemble perform pieces from current repertoire and decide whether they are in major or minor keys and why. An ideal example to use would be a musical selection that modulates into the opposite key.

The ensemble performs warm-ups in major and minor tonalities. Students try transposing a warm-up from major key to minor key and discuss what changed.

Extend the experience

A student conducts the ensemble in a selection from current repertoire by using only facial expressions or movements that express emotions. Another student conducts only the beat.

Using Mahler's Symphony no. 1, third movement, students identify major or minor keys and the name of the familiar song taken from this movement ("Frère Jacques"). They sing the song in its original major key and then sing the same song in minor key, noting what they had to change in the melody.

Related warm-ups

Following this warm-up:

- Understanding the emotional qualities of music (warm-up 73)

73 Understanding the emotional qualities of music

Materials

Musical recordings such as *An American Elegy* by Frank Ticheli and *Smetana Fanfare* by Karel Husa, or other music that expresses a wide range of emotions

Check for understanding

Ask pertinent questions: Ask students to explain how emotion is expressed in music.

Assess ability: N/A

Experience the concept

Students form groups of two. Partners create a list of various emotions and explore ways to show these emotions through facial expressions, sounds, and movements.

Students listen to *An American Elegy* by Ticheli (music written about the Columbine tragedy) and *Smetana Fanfare* by Husa and isolate musical elements that they hear, such as dynamics, tempo, accents, harmony, and direction of melody. The first partner in a group creates movement to match a musical concept, and the other partner names the emotion portrayed. Partners switch roles.

Facilitate and reflect

Why is it important to know how to express emotion creatively?

What were some of the emotions you felt and why did you feel them?

What musical strategies are used to create emotions?

What kind of emotional impact can music have on people?

Apply to ensemble/repertoire

A student conductor creates a movement that expresses an emotion. The ensemble plays a chorale warm-up (or other current warm-ups) in a style that matches the student conductor's movements. Students discuss the results.

Students find passages in current repertoire that seem to express strong emotions. They explore musical ways to interpret the passages and use their ideas as they perform them. Students then discuss whether their ideas were successful and why.

Extend the experience

Students plan a way to play one pitch either as forte or as piano. The ensemble identifies the musical concept and discusses how it can affect the emotional quality of the music. Students repeat the activity by using staccato or legato, presto or andante, and so on.

Students interpret Haiku or some other form of poetry or literature through movement and sounds.

Related warm-ups

Preceding this warm-up:

- Understanding accelerando and ritardando (warm-up 63)
- Feeling rubato (warm-up 66)
- Improving instrumental articulation (warm-up 67)
- Improving vocal articulation (warm-up 68)
- Understanding staccato and legato (warm-up 69)
- Achieving ensemble balance (warm-up 70)
- Exploring tone qualities (warm-up 71)
- Reacting to major and minor tonalities (warm-up 72)

Following this warm-up:

- Working together as an ensemble (warm-up 74)

74 Working together as an ensemble

Materials

None

Check for understanding

Ask pertinent questions: Ask students to define the term *ensemble*.

Assess ability: N/A

Experience the concept

Students explore a variety of nonlocomotor movements and synchronize several movements with a partner.

Small groups synchronize several nonlocomotor movements. They add sounds to the movements and blend the sounds to be as similar as possible.

A student leader performs a nonlocomotor movement, and the entire ensemble copies the movement. Another student creates a sound to accompany the movement. The ensemble copies the sound and movement until they are synchronized and blended.

Facilitate and reflect

What is the purpose of an ensemble in performing music?

What part does each individual play in an ensemble?

What makes an ensemble successful?

Apply to ensemble/repertoire

Each section of the ensemble performs the same portion of a current musical selection. The whole ensemble then performs the piece simultaneously, but each performer listens for another part while playing his or her own part.

The conductor separates sections into quartets of different instruments or voices. The quartets perform a selection from current literature. Students discuss the effect this exercise has on their listening abilities.

Extend the experience

The ensemble performs an entire piece of music without a conductor.

Using a selection from current repertoire that has solo parts, students take turns performing the solos.

Related warm-ups

Preceding this warm-up:

- Synchronizing ensemble beat (warm-up 3)
- Performing entrances in time (warm-up 9)
- Developing rhythmic independence (warm-up 23)
- Matching pitch (warm-up 31)
- Sculpting phrases (warm-up 52)
- Feeling rubato (warm-up 66)
- Understanding the emotional qualities of music (warm-up 73)

Possible Key Experiences

Expressing creativity in movement
Describing movement
Acting upon movement directions
Exploring the singing voice

75 Exploring vocal shapes and sounds

Materials

Choral and vocal musical recordings

Check for understanding

Ask pertinent questions: Ask students to define the term *vowel sounds.*

Assess ability: N/A

Experience the concept

Students form groups of two. The first partner in a group creates a body shape with movement. The second partner in the group copies the movement and describes it. Partners switch roles.

The first partner in a group describes a shape. The second partner in the group creates the shape with movement. Partners switch roles.

In small groups, students explore various shapes with their mouths and create sounds to go with each shape. Using the same sound, students continually change the shape of their mouths to hear how the changes affect sound.

Facilitate and reflect

How does the shape of the mouth affect the sound produced?

Compare shapes made by the body with shapes made by the mouth.

What do vowels have to do with choral or vocal sound?

Apply to ensemble/repertoire

Students breathe in and sing a vowel sound as they breathe out. They use the different mouth shapes they shared in the exploration activity in the "Experience the concept" section. As they breathe out, students add a movement to match the sound.

Students use one mouth shape to sing a selection taken from current repertoire. They sing the same music by using different mouth shapes.

Students apply mouth shapes to vowel sounds and create a handbook of warm-ups based on mouth shapes, sounds, and movements.

Extend the experience

Using a selection taken from current repertoire, students sing from one word to another without taking a breath or using a consonant. They use only vowels in a continuous phrase.

Students listen to a variety of choral or vocal musical recordings and analyze tone and vowel sounds. They create a list of suggestions for improving tone.

Related warm-ups

Preceding this warm-up:

- Matching pitch (warm-up 31)
- Improving vocal articulation (warm-up 68)
- Working together as an ensemble (warm-up 74)

Glossary

basic timing. The ability to independently feel, express, and maintain the underlying steady beat of a rhyme, song, or recorded/live musical selection with nonlocomotor and locomotor movement. This ability is the intended outcome of the key experience *feeling and expressing steady beat.*

body percussion. Creating steady beat or rhythm sounds by patting, clapping, stepping, or snapping.

Changing Directions. A collection of six CDs of international folk music (instrumental and vocal) performed by the group Gemini (Phyllis S. Weikart, creative director; High/Scope Press).

facilitate. The third teaching model component of the *Education Through Movement: Building the Foundation* program. This component of the model deals with engaging learners through action, thought, and language in many and varied ways to enable them to construct their own knowledge base.

locomotor movement. Non-anchored movement that transfers weight from one leg to the other in personal or general space, for example, stepping, walking, running, skipping, galloping, jumping; complete transfers of weight.

macrobeat. The rocking or patting beat that organizes groups of two or three microbeats; macrobeat coincides with the first beat of each group of two or three microbeats.

microbeat. The regular walking beat; each beat in a group of two or three beats.

neutral syllable. A nonsense syllable, such as *bah, ah, bum,* and so on, used to speak a rhythm.

nonlocomotor movement. Anchored movement performed in one's own space (personal space) without complete transfers of weight. Playing an instrument is a nonlocomotor movement.

pathways. Straight, curved, or zig-zag patterns on the floor or in the air that the body creates with locomotor or nonlocomotor movement (conducting patterns are specific pathways). Pathways can be used in physical education, music, art, and writing curriculum.

polyrhythms. A variety of different rhythms performed simultaneously, for example, African instrumental music.

reflection. A review or recall of concepts experienced during a lesson; transfer of concepts to other areas of the curriculum.

Rhythmically Moving. A collection of nine CDs of international folk music (instrumental and vocal) performed by the group Gemini (Phyllis S. Weikart, creative director; High/Scope Press).

SAY & DO Process. The process whereby a learner chants a word and simultaneously performs a related movement, creating a cognitive-motor link.

separate. The first teaching model component of the *Education Through Movement: Building the Foundation* program. This component of the model deals with using only one mode of presentation—visual demonstration, spoken directions, or hands-on-guidance—when presenting information to learners.

simplify. The second teaching model component of the *Education Through Movement: Building the Foundation* program. This component deals with beginning with what is easy or manageable for the learner so that students are immediately engaged at a level where they can feel successful.

synchronize. Match movements with another person or an entire group; perform the same movement at the same time.

whisper-tongue. Make a "t" sound with the mouth (with no vocal sound), as in tonguing without an instrument.

References

Carlton, E. B., & Weikart, P. S. (1994). *Foundations in elementary education: Music.* Ypsilanti, MI: High/Scope Press.

The Children's Group. (1997). *The Mozart Effect: Music for children* Vol. 3 [audio compact disc, audio cassette]. Pickering, Ontario, Canada: Author.

Marsalis, W. (1995). *Marsalis on music* [video cassette series]. New York: Sony Classical Film and Video.

Weikart, P. S. (1997). *Teaching folk dance: Successful steps.* Ypsilanti, MI: High/Scope Press.

Weikart, P. S., creative director. (1990) *Changing Directions 1–6* [audio compact discs, audio cassettes]. Ypsilanti, MI: High/Scope Press.

Weikart, P. S., creative director. (2003a). *Rhythmically moving 1–9* [audio compact discs, audio cassettes]. Ypsilanti, MI: High/Scope Press.

Weikart, P. S. (2003b). *Teaching movement & dance.* 5th Edition. Ypsilanti, MI: High/Scope Press.

Alphabetical Index of Warm-Ups

Musical Selections Provided With This Book

Al Gemali—CD 4 (3:51)

Alley Cat—RM 3 (2:19)

Corrido—RM 5 (2:52)

Danish Masquerade—CD 4 (2:37)

Debka Chag—CD 1 (2:37)

Debka Le Adama—RM 9 (2:46)

D'Hammerschmiedsg'sell'n—RM 7 (1:48)

Fjäskern—RM 2 (3:09)

Hole in the Wall—RM 4 (3:39)

Hora Hassidit—RM 5 (2:54)

Irish Washerwoman—RM 3 (3:15)

Ivanica—CD 3 (2:48)

Jessie Polka—RM 8 (5:09)

Krici Krici Ticek—CD 6 (3:08)

Mechol Hagat—RM 4 (2:57)

Mîndrele—CD 5 (3:00)

Rebetic Hasápikos—CD 6 (4:06)

Sauerländer Quadrille #5—CD 3 (2:19)

Sulam Ya'akov—CD 2 (2:37)

Tipsy—RM 6 (2:06)

Trata—CD 2 (2:31)

Tsamikos—CD 2 (3:17)

Yankee Doodle—RM 2 (1:36)

RM—*Rhythmically Moving* series of audio compact discs and cassettes

CD—*Changing Directions* series of audio compact discs and cassettes

About the Authors

Phyllis S. Weikart, Director of the Movement and Music Division, High/Scope Foundation, and developer of the program *Education Through Movement: Building the Foundation,* is a nationally known and highly respected educator-author. She bases her writing on her ongoing work with students of all ages—preschoolers to senior citizens. Her other titles include *Teaching Movement & Dance, Movement in Steady Beat,* and *Round the Circle.*

Ms. Weikart is Associate Professor Emeritus in the Division of Kinesiology, the University of Michigan, and visiting Associate Professor at the Hartt School of Music. Her formal education includes a B.S. degree from Arcadia University and an M.A. degree from the University of Michigan. In addition to being an educator and author of seven books, she is a researcher, curriculum developer, workshop leader, choreographer, and a producer of high-quality international folk dance albums (with 14 released albums). Her wide-ranging experiences have led to the development of a teaching approach that ensures teachers success with students of all ages.

Beverly Boardman, an elementary music educator with 28 years of experience in Manatee County, Florida, is the movement and music consultant for the Youth Education Division of the Florida West Coast Symphony in Sarasota. She has worked with first- through twelfth-grade students in the West Coast Symphony and as a music counselor for the High/Scope Institute for IDEAS, a month-long residential educational enrichment program for 14- to 17-year-olds.

As a field consultant for High/Scope's Movement and Music Division, Ms. Boardman presents workshops around the country for teachers in various disciplines. She is a strong advocate of active learning in a noncompetitive atmosphere in which students are free to choose, explore, and create, becoming independent thinkers and doers.

Elisabeth Bryant is Director of Music and Dean of Students in the Quabbin Regional School District in Barre, Massachusetts. Her formal education includes bachelor's and master's degrees in music with an emphasis in music education from Boston University and a master's degree in music with a concentration in clarinet performance from Northern Illinois University.

Ms. Bryant's career includes teaching graduate and undergraduate classes in music education at the University of Massachusetts, Amherst, and placing and supervising student music teachers, as well as teaching music in the Hawlemont School, which serves Charlemont and Hawley, Massachusetts. She is a field consultant for High/Scope's Movement and Music Division and the principal clarinetist and co-founder of the Massachusetts Wind Orchestra. She is also director of the Summer All-Star Band at the South Shore Conservatory in Hingham, Massachusetts, and the Quabbin Community Band in Barre, and an active clinician locally, regionally, and nationally.

Related High/Scope® Resources

Early Childhood Education

Round the Circle: Key Experiences in Movement for Young Children, 2ⁿᵈ Ed.

Young children learn through play, and their play is full of movement experiences. *Round the Circle* has been completely revised to present the *High/Scope Education Through Movement: Building the Foundation* program for preschoolers developed by Phyllis S. Weikart. This edition presents *eight key experiences in movement* that help adults *engage, enable,* and *extend* children's active movement explorations. In addition, Weikart's teaching model provides a strong framework for encouraging and supporting young children's learning. Readers will appreciate the numerous suggested activities, concrete guidelines, and effective teaching strategies that are peppered throughout the book.

BK-M1020 $24.95

P. S. Weikart. Soft cover, 176 pages. 1-57379-096-6

Movement Plus Rhymes, Songs, & Singing Games, 2ⁿᵈ Ed.

A revised collection of engaging movement activities for children. These activities supplement those described in *Round the Circle* and provide age-appropriate movement experiences. Use them during large-group time, small-group time, or transitions. **Includes CD with colorful, appropriate music to accompany activities.**

BK-M1025 $29.95

P. S. Weikart. Soft cover, CD included, 100 pages. 1-57379-066-4

Movement Plus Music: Activities for Children Ages 3 to 7, 2ⁿᵈ Ed.

Outlines movement activities for young children. Focuses on moving in coordinated ways, following directions, feeling and expressing the beat, and moving creatively. Updates many activities and suggests music from the *Rhythmically Moving 1–4* recordings.

BK-M1005 $10.95

P. S. Weikart. Soft cover, 40 pages. 0-931114-96-9

Learning on the Move Series

Movement in Steady Beat, Second Edition— Learning on the Move, Ages 3–7

The activities in this fully revised edition will keep children ages 3–7 moving to the beat and loving it! Infant/toddler caregivers as well as preschool and kindergarten teachers will find this book to be a rich source of ideas for exciting and enjoyable movement experiences for young children. **The attached CD contains rhymes (told by Phyllis Weikart) and action songs for many of the activities in the book.** An easy-to-follow plan is given for each activity and includes suggested ages, movement key experiences, curriculum concepts, materials, steps for each part of the activity, questions to extend children's understanding, and extension ideas for creative variations. Musical scores are provided for each song.

BK-M1023 $24.95

P. S. Weikart. Soft cover, CD included, 120 pages. 1-57379-130-X

85 Engaging Movement Activities—Learning on the Move, K–6 Series

The 85 activities will keep your K–6 students jogging, hopping, swaying, rocking, marching, patting, making pathways, and moving in all kinds of ways as they learn. Classroom teachers as well as specialty teachers in physical education, music, and recreation will find this book to be a rich source of ideas for challenging and enjoyable movement experiences. The experiences are planned around key curriculum concepts in movement and music as well as in academic curriculum areas such as math and reading. An easy-to-follow plan is given for each activity. **The attached music CD contains recordings that may be used with many of the activities.**

BK-E3040 $34.95

P. S. Weikart & E. B. Carlton. 216 pages, soft cover, illustrated, includes free music CD. 1-57379-125-3

To order these or any other High/Scope® products, contact High/Scope® Press: phone (800)40-PRESS fax (800)442-4FAX

To see a full listing of High/Scope® products, visit our Web site: *www.highscope.org*

Related High/Scope® Resources

For Beginners of All Ages!

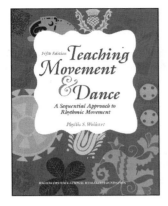

Teaching Movement & Dance: A Sequential Approach to Rhythmic Movement, 5th Ed.

Newly revised, this fifth edition includes updated information on Phyllis S. Weikart's teaching model for beginners of all ages. Also contains over 100 beginning-level dances and instructions for introducing movement and dance in understandable and enjoyable ways. Music for the dances is recorded on the *Rhythmically Moving 1–9* recordings.

BK-M1022 $34.95

P. S. Weikart. Soft cover, 450 pages. 1-57379-132-6

Guides to Rhythmically Moving 1–5

These guides are the first in the *Rhythmically Moving 1–9* series. Each guide lists the title, band, length, and origin for each *Rhythmically Moving* musical selection. Each guide also indicates whether the selection is vocal or instrumental, the major instruments played, and the number of repetitions of the selection. Guides include suggested activities for each selection.

Guide to Rhythmically Moving 1
BK-M1009 $12.95
E. B. Carlton and P. S. Weikart. Soft cover, 60 pages. 1-57379-004-4

Guide to Rhythmically Moving 2
BK-M1011 $12.95
E. B. Carlton and P. S. Weikart. Soft cover, 72 pages. 1-57379-015-X

Guide to Rhythmically Moving 3
BK-M1014 $12.95
E. B. Carlton and P. S. Weikart. Soft cover, 76 pages. 1-57379-028-1

Guide to Rhythmically Moving 4
BK-M1015 $12.95
E. B. Carlton and P. S. Weikart. Soft cover, 70 pages. 1-57379-049-4

Guide to Rhythmically Moving 5
BK-M1021 $12.95
E. B. Carlton and P. S. Weikart. Soft cover, 82 pages, 2001. 1-57379-102-4

Music for Students of All Ages

Rhythmically Moving 1–9

Music for students of all ages. Includes suggestions for use with *Teaching Movement & Dance: A Sequential Approach to Rhythmic Movement*. Can also be used with the *Beginning Folk Dances Illustrated* video series and all other folk dance books from High/Scope® Press as well as the early childhood movement and music publications. Select one or all of these recordings. There is no special order or level of difficulty. Call us or visit our Web site for complete song lists.

P. S. Weikart, creative director. CDs.

Rhythmically Moving 1
BK-M2401 $15.95 1-57379-185-7

Rhythmically Moving 2
BK-M2402 $15.95 1-57379-138-5

Rhythmically Moving 3
BK-M2403 $15.95 1-57379-142-3

Rhythmically Moving 4
BK-M2404 $15.95 1-57379-148-2

Rhythmically Moving 5
BK-M2405 $15.95 1-57379-149-0

Rhythmically Moving 6
BK-M2406 $15.95 1-57379-175-X

Rhythmically Moving 7
BK-M2407 $15.95 1-57379-176-8

Rhythmically Moving 8
BK-M2408 $15.95 1-57379-177-6

Rhythmically Moving 9
BK-M2409 $15.95 1-57379-178-4

Related High/Scope® Resources

High/Scope® brings you the joy of movement and music

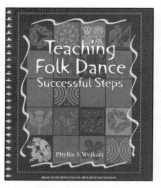

Teaching Folk Dance: Successful Steps

This comprehensive guide to both beginning and intermediate folk dance will help teachers introduce dances to students of all ages. This book consolidates and expands on the material presented in Phyllis S. Weikart's two landmark teaching manuals, *Teaching Movement & Dance: A Sequential Approach to Rhythmic Movement,* and *Teaching Movement & Dance: Intermediate Folk Dance.* This is an essential resource for teachers of music, elementary and secondary education, physical education, and special education, and for persons working with senior citizens.

BK-M1012 $49.95
P. S. Weikart. Soft cover, 728 pages. 1-57379-008-7

Dance Notations—Teaching Folk Dance: Successful Steps

Cards providing a quick reference to dance descriptions and music for all dances in *Teaching Folk Dance.*

BK-M4902 $49.95
Set of 245 cards plus metal ring fastener. 1-57379-039-7

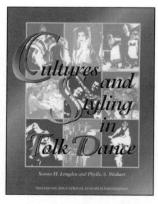

Cultures and Styling in Folk Dance

This extraordinary book by Sanna H. Longden and Phyllis S. Weikart is filled with rich background discussions on the more than 200 dances in Phyllis S. Weikart's musical collections and dance textbooks. Covers each dance's history, choreographic origins, ethnic instruments and music, and traditional clothing and costumes, and contains helpful teaching suggestions.

BK-M1017 $37.95
S. Longden and P. S. Weikart, soft cover, photos, 408 pages. 1-57379-016-8

Teaching Folk Dance: Successful Steps 1— A Teaching Videotape

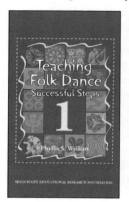

Watch as Phyllis S. Weikart teaches nine different beginning folk dances to an engaging group of fourth-graders! The dances use even and uneven stepping patterns and are taught in a motor-development progression from simple to more complex. Includes helpful teaching strategies that can be used to ensure success with students ages 7 to senior citizens.

BK-M4006 $39.95
Color videotape, 102 minutes, 1-57379-038-9

Teaching Folk Dance: Successful Steps 2— A Teaching Videotape

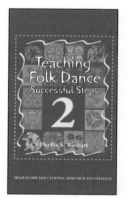

Once again, Phyllis S. Weikart demonstrates her highly successful teaching process—this time to an eager group of high school students. The ten dances on this video use even and uneven beginning folk dance steps and follow the simple-to-more-complex motor-development progression. This video, with its helpful teaching suggestions, can be used with students ages 9 to senior citizens.

BK-M4007 $39.95
Color videotape, 127 minutes, 1-57379-081-8